Her Master's in Teesdale

Grassholme Reservoir from Harter Fell.

I've wandered many a weary mile,
And in strange countries been;
I've dwelt in towns and on wild moors,
And curious sights I've seen;
But still my heart clings to the dale
Where Tees rolls to the sea,
Compared with what I've seen I'll say
The Teesdale hills for me.

Richard Watson (1833-1891)
'The Teesdale Poet'

Her Master's Walks in Teesdale

Stephen I. Robinson

BARLEY · PUBLISHING
2010

Barley Publishing
10 Mill Green View
Swarcliffe
Leeds LS14 5JT
www.hm-walks.co.uk

First published 2010

© S. I. Robinson 2010

ISBN 978-1-898550-06-8

Drawings by Andrew Haddelsey
Maps and photographs by Stephen I. Robinson

Maps reproduced by permission of Ordnance Survey on behalf of
The Controller of Her Majesty's Stationery Office
© Crown Copyright 100016545.

All rights reserved.
No part of this publication may be reproduced,
stored in a retrieval system or transmitted,
in any form or any means, electronic,
mechanical, photocopying, recording or otherwise,
without the prior written permission of the copyright owner.

Printed in Great Britain by:
Aspire Print Solutions Ltd
Unit 9, Enterprise Court,
Pit Lane, Garforth, Leeds LS25 4BU
Telephone 0113 287 5141

Holwick.

Contents

Paw-word	6
Introduction	7
Be Prepared	8
About the Walks	9
The Walks	
1 Widdybank Fell and Cauldron Snout	10
2 High Force and Holwick Scars	14
3 Hardberry Hill and Hudeshope Beck	18
4 Lunedale and Harter Fell	22
5 Baldersdale and Cotherstone Moor	26
6 Eggleston Bridge and Romaldkirk	30
7 Lartington and Deepdale	34
8 Bowes, Deepdale and God's Bridge	38
9 Egglestone Abbey and Greta Bridge	42
10 Sudburn Beck and Staindrop Moor	46
Glossary	50
The Country Code	51
Information Desk	52
Acknowledgements	Inside back cover

Paw-word

Where's the master got to? We should have been on our way by this time. It's the same every weekend, he makes plans, but something always seems to delay him. Unlike me – just mention the magic word, *'walk'*, and I'm ready in seconds.

Who's that man coming through our gate? Another pizza menu! Not if I can help it. *Grrrr, grrrr, woof, woof, grrrr.* That's seen him off. 'RINGO!! Come here NOW!' Aah, at last! The master's here, he sounds a bit stressed, he must be anxious to get going. I always look forward to the weekends, we normally travel into the countryside to undertake one of *'his'* walks. They are usually very enjoyable, but I'm at a loss to understand why he stops so much. He makes notes and takes photographs of just about everything we pass.

On one occasion we came across a small flock of Swaledales in a churchyard and he decided to take a picture. He actually talked to one of the sheep saying, 'Please Mrs Swale, don't move.' Later, in a woodland clearing he managed to photograph a red squirrel and then he said, 'Go on little fella, move a bit further along the branch.' Perhaps he aspires to be the famous Doctor Dolittle or, more likely, he's totally flipped his lid. The amazing thing is – both the sheep and the squirrel did as he asked, very strange!

Another fascinating thing is that bag which he carries on his back. It holds everything we need during our walk and also many other items that are seldom required including sun tan lotion and Kendal mint cake, ugh! That bag has to be bigger on the inside – could it be a smaller version of the *Tardis?* Just a minute, isn't that evil archenemy of the *Doctor* called the *Master?!*

Introduction

Teesdale is revered as one of the most beautiful and spectacular areas in England. It is a peaceful, unspoilt landscape, richly endowed with natural beauty and provides an incredible feeling of solitude and tranquility.

In 1988 the whole of Upper Teesdale was included in the designation for the North Pennines Area of Outstanding Natural Beauty (AONB). It stretches across 772 square miles (2000km^2) and takes in parts of County Durham, Cumbria and Northumbria. The area is well known for its diversity of wildlife and scenic excellence, but it also has a unique geological heritage. In 2003, in recognition of these special qualities, the North Pennines became the first area in Britain to be awarded the status of UNESCO European and Global Geopark - stressing its global importance.

The river Tees, from which the dale takes its name, rises on the bleak eastern slopes of Cross Fell, England's second highest mountain with a height of 2930 feet (893m). The river's name is thought to have originated from the ancient Welsh *Tes* which means 'sunshine or heat' and translates as the 'boiling or surging river'. Although the flow of the Tees is subdued by Cow Green Reservoir, it fits this description admirably. Cauldron Snout, England's largest cascade, is just below the dam and, seven miles (11.25km) downstream, England's largest waterfall, High Force, thunders 70 feet (21m) into a deep pool.

These magnificent falls owe their existence to the Whin Sill, or dolerite as it is correctly known. Dolerite is a hard igneous rock which played a prominent role in the surface geology and scenery of Teesdale. It formed 295 million years ago when magma oozed up through fractures in the earlier Carboniferous rocks, spreading out between the layers of limestone, sandstone and shale. The magma cooled and solidified into a huge sheet of igneous rock, reaching thicknesses of up to 230 feet (70m). Although the Whin Sill has suffered erosion and weathering spanning millions of years it is only partly exposed at the surface.

The high fells of the North Pennines have encouraged a cooler, almost sub-arctic climate, perfect conditions for ensuring the survival of the rare spring gentian and the Teesdale violet. Bird's-eye primrose and many other important species such as butterwort, mountain pansy, rockrose and spring sandwort are also well established. According to tradition it is bad luck to bring a gentian into the house as you stand the chance of being struck by lightning! *The solution to this is very simple – DO NOT PICK THE FLOWERS! – Any of them!!*

Wildlife abounds here and the region is home to 80 per cent of England's black grouse population. Other breeding birds include curlew, snipe, dunlin, oystercatcher, redshank and moorland raptors such as merlin and short-eared owl. Roe deer, fox and smaller mammals like the hare, stoat and weasel are common, but the polecat is less frequent. Red squirrel and otter are the icing on the cake for those who are lucky enough to spot them.

This is a superb place for walkers, especially those who enjoy wilder, secluded areas. It has a substantial network of footpaths and bridle-ways, providing access to an excellent choice of routes ranging from easy riverside rambles to strenuous fell walks. Since the introduction of the Countryside and Rights of Way Act 2000 (CRoW), often called the 'right to roam', route permutations are limitless. However, walkers should check for any restrictions before setting out if their route ventures onto open access land, especially when they are accompanied by one of our four-legged friends. All of the routes in this guide are on public rights of way and therefore do not have any dog restrictions.

Teesdale is a feast of delights, providing wonderful opportunities for visitors, with a host of outdoor activities including angling, bird watching, canoeing, cycling, pony trekking, sailing, water skiing, wind surfing and much more. Your visit will leave you energised and uplifted, with just one wish – to return! And I'm sure that you will.

Stephen I. Robinson,
March 2010

Be Prepared!

Walking, arguably the most enjoyable of outdoor pastimes and undoubtedly one of the healthiest, can be tailored to meet the requirements of almost anyone.

Your preference might be for a gentle stroll of three to four miles along a quiet riverbank or woodland path, or perhaps a strenuous hill walk of ten miles or more. Whichever you choose, provided you are properly equipped, your walk will not only be much safer but also more enjoyable. This does not mean taking everything including the kitchen sink! If you are a keen photographer a camera with spare films or memory card is essential. Binoculars are mandatory for birdwatchers. The artist needs his sketchbook and pencil. But please remember, everything you take is extra weight that has to be carried.

What to wear and carry will depend on the season, the weather and good sense. The items in the following lists are recommended, but think carefully about what to take. Some extra items may be needed on a hill walk which could be left behind when walking through the lower meadows. Due to our unpredictable climate, however, a spare wool sweater and waterproofs should always be carried.

TO WEAR

Strong walking boots or stout shoes

Thick woollen socks (two pairs)

Cotton shirt or T-Shirt

Walking breeches, trousers or shorts (Jeans are not advisable, they lose their heat retention when wet)

Woollen hat, balaclava or sun hat

TO CARRY

A small rucksack, thirty to forty litres in capacity, to carry the following items:

Waterproof anorak or cagoule

Wool sweater or fibre pile jacket

Gloves, scarf

First aid kit, compass, whistle

Torch, pencil and note pad

Ordnance Survey map of the area

Emergency rations, survival bag

Water bottle with water

Food and snacks

High visibility vest (wear in poor light and during shooting season on grouse moors)

OPTIONAL ITEMS

Camera and spare films or memory card

GPS

Binoculars

Swiss army knife

Flask with tea, coffee, soup or other hot beverage

Waterproof over-trousers, gaiters

Five to ten yards (or metres) of thin cord (Useful for temporary laces etc.)

Langdon Beck.

About the Walks

These routes provide a stunning introduction to the glorious and diverse Teesdale landscape. They embrace a wide range of habitats; wild heather moors, flower-rich hay meadows, rough pasture, spectacular river and woodland scenery.

All of the walks follow circular routes ranging from 6 to 8¼ miles (9.6 to 13.3km). They begin from a car park where one is available, or at a place where it is possible to park safely without blocking farm gateways or causing inconvenience to others.

Final surveys of the routes were carried out during summer and autumn 2009 and the maps amended accordingly. However, from time to time walls, fences and hedges may be removed, stiles and gates resited, new forestry plantations established and buildings may have been demolished. For this reason it is recommended that the relevant Ordnance Survey maps and a compass are taken with you. These will help to determine landmarks and locate alternative routes where necessary.

The relevant area of the map has been used and then simplified so that only the walls, fences, buildings, rivers, roads and landmarks etc., where the track passes through are included.

Each map has the route marked in red with numbered arrow pointers for each section of the walk. These relate to the descriptive guide on the facing page, which also includes a grid reference for the starting point of each stage. When used together these features should help to avoid confusion, but common sense and some rudimentary map reading experience would be advantageous.

The time given for the completion of each walk is approximate and does not include any allowance for lunch breaks, photo stops or sightseeing. As a rule of thumb, adding one third of the stated time for stops should be sufficient. If you are accompanied by young children extra walking time will have to be allowed. Extended stays at any of the inns or tea shops en route will also have to be added to the time.

WIDDYBANK FELL and CAULDRON SNOUT

FROM COW GREEN RESERVOIR 7¾ MILES (12.5KM)

Upper Teesdale is renowned for its beautiful scenery and this circuit of Widdybank Fell endorses that opinion. The rich variety of flora and fauna should be sufficient to satisfy the most demanding of naturalists.

Before leaving the car park take a little time to look around and absorb the magnificent panorama. Cow Green Reservoir stretches across the view, with the high summits of the Pennine hills providing a stunning backdrop. To the left, beyond the dam, stands Mickle Fell which rises to 2488 feet (758m); looking directly across the reservoir is Meldon Hill at 2517 feet (767m); panning right is Great Dun Fell at 2783 feet (848m) which is easy to recognise with the radar installation perched on its summit; next is Little Dun Fell which is a mere 20 feet (6m) lower; then Cross Fell, the highest peak on the Pennine ridge at 2930 feet (893m).

Cow Green Reservoir opened in 1971 after protests to prevent it's construction had failed. It was built to ensure a constant supply of water to the thirsty industries of Teesside, more than 50 miles (80km) away. When filled to capacity the reservoir holds 9000 million gallons (41,000 million litres). The dam is 1875 feet (571m) long and 82 feet (25m) high. Before the reservoir was built the course of the river Tees made a large crescent, known as 'The Weel', where it gathered force before plummeting down the spectacular staircase of Cauldron Snout.

The route from Weelhead Sike provides sweeping views across the valley to Chapelfell Top and Fendrith Fell, helping to compensate for the somewhat hard surface underfoot. To the right is the wild heather moorland of Widdybank Fell. Here, in the spring and early summer, you may see the golden plover, recognised by its golden-brown back with black speckles and a black belly. Curlew, lapwing, meadow pipit and skylark are also common during the breeding season.

Leaving the road we follow a good track to Widdybank Farm and the prominent outcrop of Cronkley Scar comes into view. In the mid-nineteenth century, an area of shale found in the rocks at Cronkley Scar proved to be suitable for making pencils. A pencil mill was built nearby which operated until 1899. The pencils, known locally as 'widdies', were produced by grinding the shale into a powder and then compressing it into moulds.

After reaching the banks of the river Tees, a broad track leads upstream to the towering crags at Falcon Clints. Golden eagles once soared above these rocky cliffs and their eyries remain, waiting for them to return! Our path winds its way through the rocks at the foot of the cliffs where lichens and mosses are well established; lady fern, wood anemone, wood horsetail and woolly hair moss shelter in the fallen rocks. The rippling of the river is the only sound disturbing the solitude.

Further upstream we reach a confluence where Maize Beck merges with the river Tees. Prior to 1974 this marked the boundaries of three counties; below the juncture, the Tees separated County Durham from the North Riding of Yorkshire; above the juncture, it separated County Durham from Westmorland, which is now part of Cumbria.

Our path continues along the riverside and the sound of crashing water grows louder with each step. Suddenly, we are confronted with the spectacular waterfall of Cauldron Snout, once described as 'a cascade of torrential wildness'. Here the Tees plunges, in a series of cataracts, down a rocky staircase 600 feet (183m) in length. The vertical drop from the first cataract to the last is 200 feet (61m) – England's largest cascade waterfall. Nowadays the Cow Green dam controls the river's flow, releasing enough to make an impressive display most of the time. However, when the reservoir is full, curtains of water spill over and quickly surge into an awesome force, reminiscent of its former magnificence.

According to local folklore the area near the falls is haunted by the ghost of the 'Singing Lady'. A young Victorian farm girl fell in love with a local lead miner, but the affair ended when the miner returned home to his family. Overcome with grief the girl made her way to the edge of the falls where she threw herself into the raging torrent. It is said that her spirit can be seen, on cold moonlit nights, sitting on a rock near the falls where she sadly laments the loss of her lover.

After an invigorating climb to the top of Cauldron Snout, the concrete wall of Cow Green Dam appears. But the views quickly improve and can be enjoyed during our return to the car park.

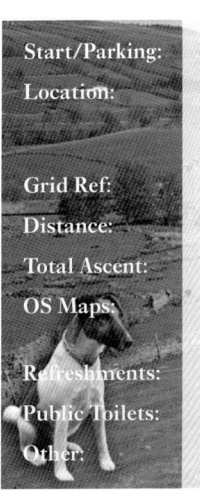

Start/Parking:	Weelhead Sike car park at Cow Green Reservoir.
Location:	Follow the B6277 Alston Road from Middleton-in-Teesdale for 7¼ miles (12.2km) to the Langdon Beck Hotel. Turn left and follow minor road for 3 miles (4.5km) to Cow Green Reservoir.
Grid Ref:	NY 811 309. Postcode: for Langdon Beck Hotel - DL12 0XP.
Distance:	7¾ miles (12.5km) circular. Allow 4 hrs walking time.
Total Ascent:	531 feet (162m) Maximum Elevation: 1679 feet (512m).
OS Maps:	Explorer OL31 (1:25,000), Landranger 91 (1:50,000) or Landranger 92 (1:50,000).
Refreshments:	None en route, nearest Langdon Beck Hotel.
Public Toilets:	None en route, nearest High Force.
Other:	Bus service passes through Langdon Beck.

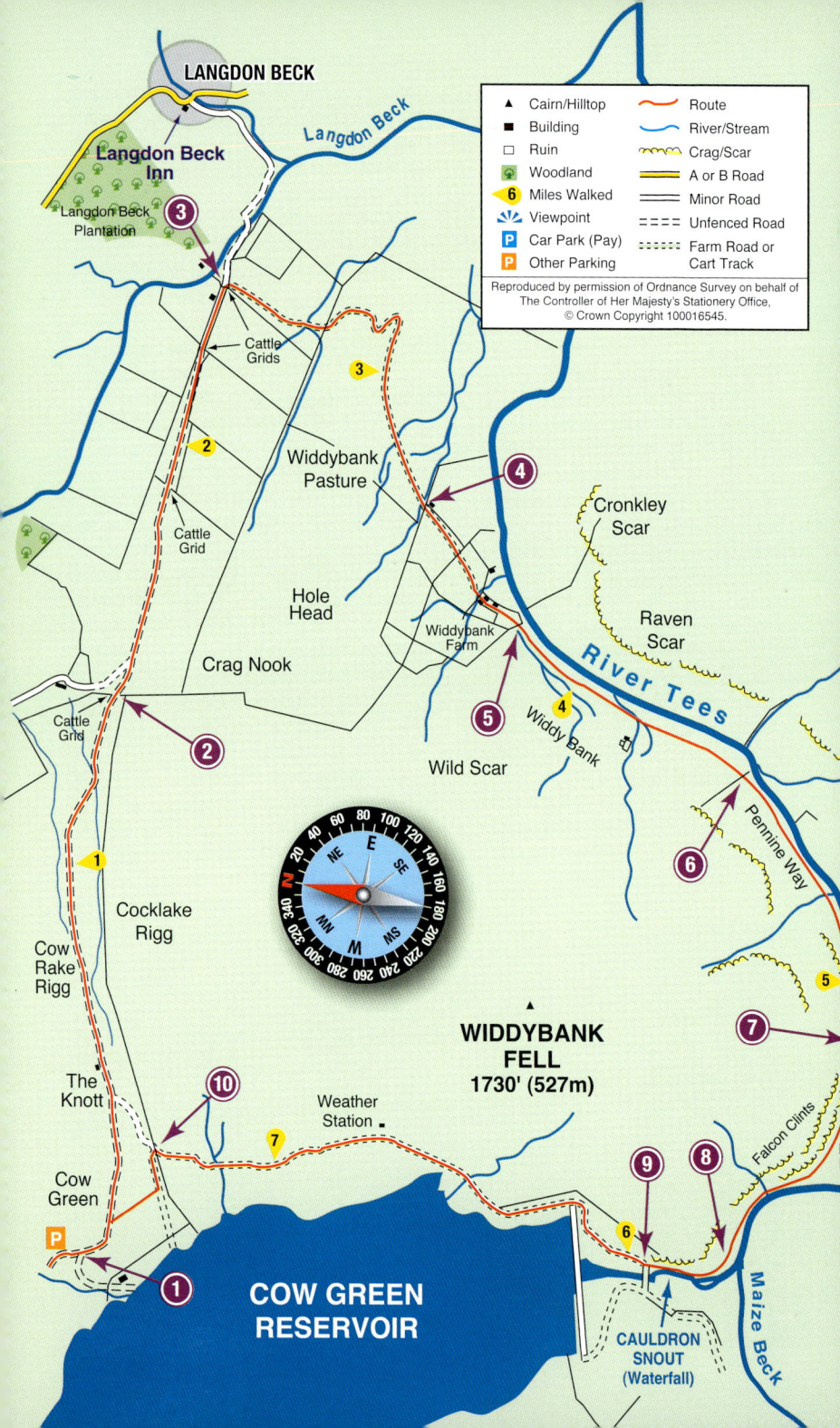

Widdybank Fell and Cauldron Snout

① *(GR: 811 309)* From the car park turn left and follow the tarmacked road heading back towards Langdon Beck.

② *(GR: 832 311)* Go through the gate beside the cattle grid and descend to the road junction. Turn right and continue along the road via three more gates/cattle grids.

③ *(GR: 847 310)* Leave the road via a gate on the right *(SP Public Footpath)* and follow a stony farm track. Go through a gate near an English Nature notice board and continue along the stony track which leads over Widdybank Pasture.

④ *(GR: 841 301)* Go through a gate and continue across two fields to reach Widdybank Farm. Pass to the left of the farmhouse and then head towards a stone step-stile in the far left corner of the field.

⑤ *(GR: 837 296)* Cross the stile and continue on a clear track following the river Tees upstream.

⑥ *(GR: 833 287)* Go through the gate and continue along the riverside. Some sections are a little rocky and involve a bit of a scramble but there are wooden walkways and stone flags over the boggier parts. In wet weather the rocks and boulders are extremely slippery so please take extra care.

⑦ *(GR: 824 281)* Leave the riverside temporarily and follow a clear path, mainly flags and wooden walkways, below Falcon Clints. After rejoining the river Tees continue upstream to its confluence with Maize Beck.

⑧ *(GR: 816 284)* Follow the river round to the right where Cauldron Snout comes into view. Climb up a rocky path to the right of the falls, take extra care, the path can be very slippery even in dry weather.

⑨ *(GR: 814 287)* Turn right onto a tarmacked road and follow it uphill to the right of the dam. Remain on the road as it winds its way around Cow Green Reservoir and continue past a weather station.

⑩ *(GR: 815 307)* Go through the gate and turn left onto a stony track. Follow this for about 100 yards (91m) and turn right onto a narrower track which leads up to the tarmacked road used at the beginning of the walk. Turn left and return to the car park.

Cauldron Snout and the river Tees.

HIGH FORCE and HOLWICK SCARS

FROM BOWLEES 7¾ MILES (12.5KM)

This walk begins with a refreshing stroll by the riverside, where a wide variety of wild flowers and birds can be enjoyed. Then a rugged moorland trek unveils some of Teesdale's impressive scenery.

The Bowlees Visitor Centre, situated in a converted chapel, was founded in 1976 by the Durham Wildlife Trust. Well laid out displays explain the wildlife and special landscape of Teesdale. The centre also provides an insight into the way of life in the Dale and stresses the need for conservation.

From Bowlees our route delivers us to the river Tees at Wynch Bridge. This narrow bridge was built in 1830, replacing an earlier flimsy structure dating back to 1741. The bridge is sometimes called 'Two-inch Bridge' due to its diminutive size. It is suspended by two strong chains across a rocky gorge and is enriched by beautiful river scenery. The original bridge is claimed to have been the first suspension bridge in Europe. It was damaged by the great flood of 1771 and finally collapsed in 1802 when eleven people were crossing, one man being killed.

Just upstream from the bridge are the scenic falls of Low Force, also known as Salmon Leap. The Tees used to be one of the finest salmon rivers in the country, with migratory salmon once reaching the pool at High Force. The river has suffered severe pollution in the past, attributed mainly to industry and urban development. Since the 1970s the water quality has improved substantially and salmon are now returning to the upper reaches.

As we continue upstream there are many opportunities to see Teesdale's wildlife in close-up. Outcrops of sugar limestone provide the perfect habitat for many rare wild flowers, including bird's-eye primrose which is easily recognised by its exquisite lilac-pink flowers and yellow centres. Alpine bistort, globeflower and several species of orchid are also well established. In the breeding season wading birds, such as the common sandpiper, can be spotted on the riverside cobbles and the adjacent hay meadows are home to curlew, lapwing and snipe.

After a short climb from Holwick Head Bridge we reach the Moor House Nature Reserve. The reserve encloses 18,250 acres (7387ha) of upland habitats, from lower lying hay meadows and rough pasture to blanket bogs and summit heaths of the high fells. It also contains the largest juniper wood in England. Although it has declined in many places, due to agricultural needs, juniper is a priority for conservation in this area. The berries were once prized for their medicinal powers and were claimed to be effective for coughs, gout, sciatica and kidney disorders. They were also used as a flavouring for bread, cakes and gin.

The thunderous roar of High Force will soon be heard and then the dramatic waterfall is revealed, crashing 70 feet (21m) into a deep, dark pool. High Force, regarded as England's biggest waterfall, actually consists of two falls, flowing on either side of a central rock, but the northern fall is only seen in action after periods of heavy rainfall. In March 1881, after a rapid thaw, the river became a raging torrent and High Force engulfed the central rock in a single waterfall. The river's flow is now regulated by the Cow Green dam, and such events are unlikely. But the falls still leave an awe-inspiring impression.

Further upstream we part company with the riverside to climb the slopes of Bracken Rigg. The scenery is spectacular; the river Tees meanders through a beautiful gorge below, and in the distance the whitewashed buildings of Forest-in-Teesdale glisten. We descend from the crest to join a broad, grassy track known as the Green Trod. Until the 1890s this was one of the main drovers' routes from Scotland. It provided a vital link to the industrial towns of Yorkshire, which required vast quantities of fresh meat in order to feed their growing populations.

Whatever its former use, the Green Trod is ideal for our purpose, providing us with tremendous views of Teesdale as we make our way to Holwick. Until 1974, when the county boundaries were changed, Holwick was the most northerly village in Yorkshire. Today it is a peaceful hamlet, straggling the roadside beneath the towering whinstone crags of Holwick Scars. However, it was a much larger community in the nineteenth century when it had a busy lead mining industry.

We continue to Scoberry Bridge, another narrow footbridge crossing the Tees. From here a good path leads through lush meadows returning us to Bowlees.

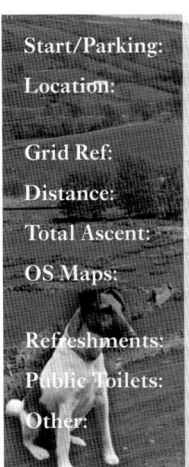

Start/Parking:	Bowlees Visitor Centre car park.
Location:	The Bowlees Visitor Centre is situated about 3½ miles (5.6km) north-west of Middleton-in-Teesdale on the B6277 Alston Road.
Grid Ref:	NY 907 282. Postcode: DL12 0XE.
Distance:	7¾ miles (12.5km) circular. Allow 4 hrs walking time.
Total Ascent:	696 feet (212m) Maximum Elevation: 1352 feet (412m).
OS Maps:	Explorer OL31 (1:25,000) or Landranger 91 (1:50,000) or Landranger 92 (1:50,000).
Refreshments:	High Force Hotel and the Strathmore Arms at Holwick.
Public Toilets:	Bowlees and High Force, none en route.
Other:	Bus service, visitor centre and nature trail, there is also a Methodist chapel at Newbiggin.

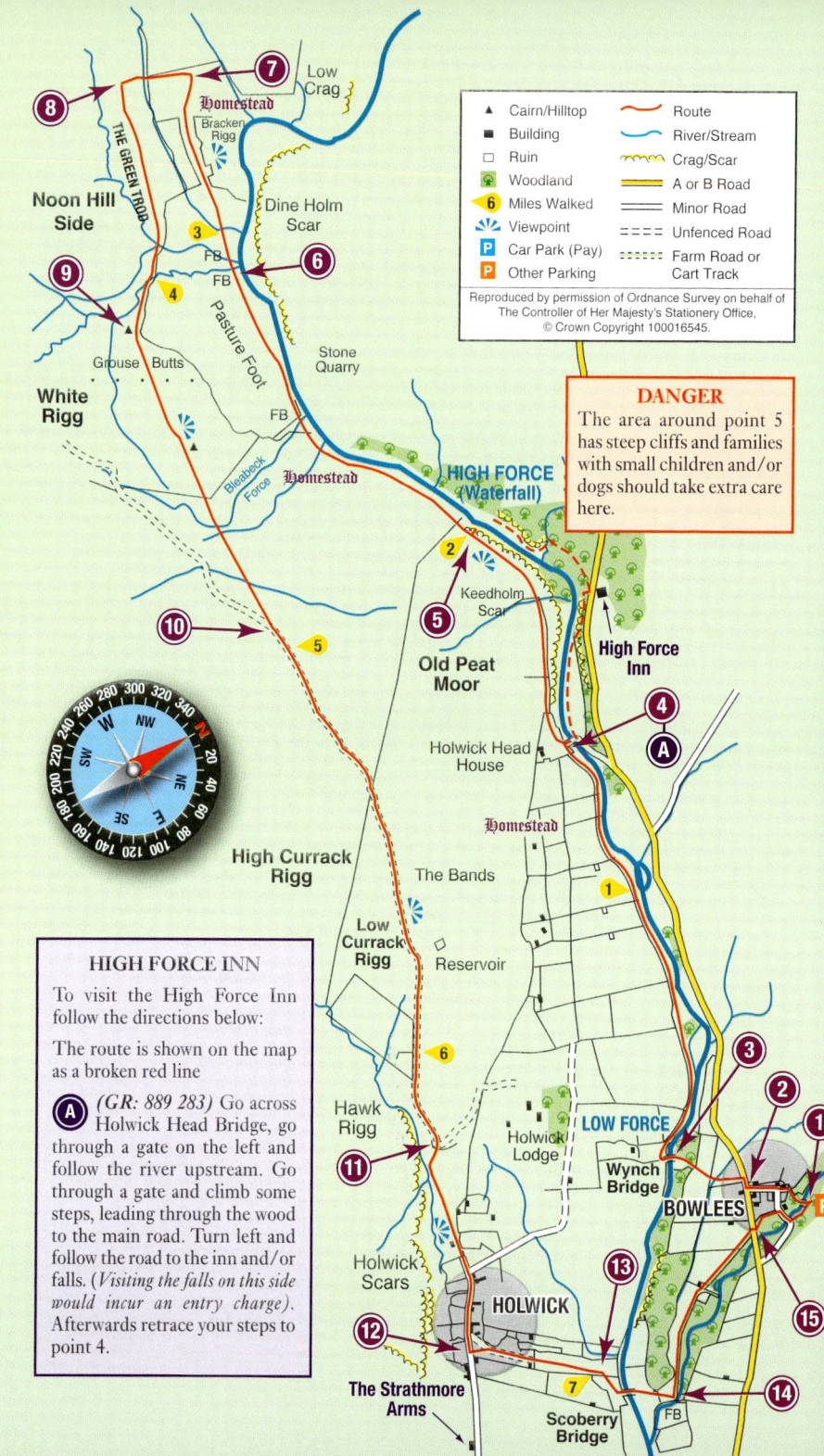

High Force and Holwick Scars

① *(GR: 907 282)* Leave the car park via the footbridge over Bowlees Beck and follow a clear path to the Bowlees Visitor Centre. Pass to the left of the centre and go through a gate. Continue along the lane to the main road.

② *(GR: 906 281)* Turn right, after a few yards cross the road and go through the gate opposite *(SP Public Footpath Wynch Bridge)*. Follow a clear path across two fields. Go through a gap-stile and descend through the woodland to Wynch Bridge.

③ *(GR: 904 279)* Cross the bridge and turn right, climb up slightly and join a clear path. Continue past a sheep sculpture and follow the river Tees upstream, crossing several stone step-stiles to reach Holwick Head Bridge.

④ *(GR: 889 283)* Continue ahead, climbing gradually along a paved path and go through a gate into the Moor House Nature Reserve. The path soon levels out and remains well defined as it passes through a forest of juniper bushes.

⑤ *(GR: 881 284)* Turn right and after a few yards the thundering falls of High Force are visible. Return to the track and continue upstream, cross a footbridge and go past a stone quarry sited on the opposite bank of the river.

⑥ *(GR: 869 281)* Go over two footbridges and bear left away from the riverside. Cross a stream and follow a paved path/wooden gantry leading up the slope ahead. Continue between fenced juniper bushes to a marker post on Bracken Rigg.

⑦ *(GR: 862 283)* Turn left *(marker post GT)* and descend to a gate in the bottom corner. Continue to a junction of paths near a Nature Reserve sign.

⑧ *(GR: 860 280)* Turn left to follow the Green Trod descending slightly and heading towards the wall on the left. After crossing a stream, climb steeply alongside the wall, heading towards a cairn on the hillside.

⑨ *(GR: 868 276)* Go past the cairn. The path soon levels out and passes through a line of grouse butts. Continue across open moorland passing a prominent cairn sited on a small hill. Go through a gate and continue through the pasture crossing several small streams, eventually arriving at a rough stone track.

⑩ *(GR: 880 275)* Turn left onto the track and follow it through a gate, descending to a sharp left bend where we reach another sheep sculpture, doubling as a step-stile.

⑪ *(GR: 899 272)* Leave the track via the step-stile. Climb up for a few yards and then turn left to follow a track descending beside Holwick Scars. Go through a gate and continue to join the main road at Holwick. Continue straight ahead along the road.

⑫ *(GR: 906 269)* Leave the road via a stile on the left *(SP Public Footpath)*, descend through two fields. Near the bottom of the second field turn right and go through a stone step-stile in the wall.

⑬ *(GR: 909 273)* Bear half left and go over a wooden step-stile in the fence. Descend some steps and cross Scoberry Bridge. Continue directly across the field passing to the right of a derelict barn, descend slightly towards a footbridge. But, **DON'T CROSS IT!**

⑭ *(GR: 911 275)* Turn left and follow the wall through two fields. Pass to the right of a farmhouse via two gates and then follow a good farm lane to the main road.

⑮ *(GR: 908 280)* Cross the road and go through the gate opposite *(SP Public Footpath)*. Follow a clear path through the wood and go through a gap-stile. Turn right and follow the road over a bridge, turn left *(sign Car Park)* and return to the car park.

THE SHEEP SCULPTURES

Two impressive sculptures are passed during the walk. The first, near Low Force, shows sheep walking along a drystone wall and expresses the views of 'a walker' and 'a farmer'. The second, near Holwick Scars, is a monumental step-stile. This is supported by two carved, stone sheep and columns with red grouse nestling in the clay-coloured capitals. The step is inscribed with the words 'Moor or Less'. The sculptures were carved mainly on site and are the work of Keith Alexander of Barnard Castle.

HARDBERRY HILL and HUDESHOPE BECK

FROM MIDDLETON-IN-TEESDALE 7½ MILES (12.1 KM)

Teesdale's industrial heritage is just as enticing as its scenery and this walk has a good mixture of the two. The woodland around Hudeshope Beck sustains a rich variety of wildlife and makes a wonderful finish to the walk.

Middleton-in-Teesdale, revered as the 'capital' of Upper Teesdale, lies in the very heart of the most beautiful and enchanting scenery that can be imagined. It was founded *c.*1031, when King Cnut granted it, as part of a much larger estate, to the monks of St Cuthbert at Durham. However, it did not begin to grow significantly until the nineteenth century when it became an important lead mining centre.

In 1815 the Quaker-owned London Lead Company established their northern headquarters at Middleton. They built houses, schools and libraries for their workers and became the first British company to introduce the five day working week. Water was piped to convenient points around the village and some of the original tap housings can still be seen in the walls. Every house had its own vegetable garden and some even boasted a purpose-built pigsty at the back door.

The Parish church, dedicated to St Mary, the Virgin, was rebuilt *c.*1878. It has several medieval grave-covers built into the interior of the north wall. The east window of the original church is now erected in the churchyard. One of the most interesting features of the church is its detached bell-tower, the only one of its kind in the Diocese of Durham. This was built about 1557 to house three bells bequeathed by William Bell, 'prest and parson of Middleton in Tesdaill'. The bells are reputed to have been pealed by one man who used both hands and one of his feet.

Our route from Middleton follows a quiet road which has tremendous panoramic views of Teesdale. The river Tees meanders along the valley floor with the impressive Holwick Scars as a backdrop. The vista improves further when we leave the road to begin our ascent of Hardberry Hill. To the west stands Great Dun Fell, easily identified by the radar station on its summit, right of this is Little Dun Fell and then Cross Fell, the highest peak on the Pennine ridge.

After crossing the shoulder of Hardberry Hill the harsher scenery of the lead mining period becomes more apparent. The valley is strewn with the remains of the Coldberry Mine which closed in 1955 after more than 200 years of lead production. Coldberry was one of the largest lead mining complexes in the North Pennines. The immediate area of the mines has been granted the status of a Scheduled Ancient Monument.

The most prominent scar is Coldberry Gutter, the result of an early open-cast mining technique known as 'hushing'. This involved the construction of a reservoir with a turf dam on the moor above the suspected vein. When the reservoir was full, the dam was breeched so that the sudden torrent swept down, tearing away the soil and surface rocks to expose the vein. Then picks and crowbars were used to loosen and remove the ore. This process was carried out repeatedly, creating deep gullies on the hillside which are visible from many miles around.

During the descent, remnants of a water balance system can be seen. This consisted of a wheeled water-tank which moved down an incline between two walls. A rope from the tank was attached to a bucket of ore in the shaft and, as the tank went down, the bucket came up. Using the weight of water to raise the ore from the shaft was both economical and energy efficient.

Leaving behind the ravages of the mines we descend gradually to Hudeshope Beck. The scenery quickly begins to improve and there are excellent views across Teesdale with the distinctive wooded crest of Kirkcarrion in the distance.

As we approach the Miners' Bridge the well preserved Skears kilns come into view. These impressive kilns date from 1840 when the first pair were built, a second pair was added later in that century and a single semi-circular kiln was added in the early twentieth century. The final kiln, which has now collapsed, was built in 1941 to help satisfy the larger demand for lime during World War II. Limestone from the nearby Skears Quarry was burnt here and the lime extracted was used mainly to help neutralise acidic soils. The kilns remained in production until 1960.

From the kilns we follow a pleasant lane alongside the beck passing the attractive Horseshoe Falls. The lane leads back onto the road and returns us Middleton.

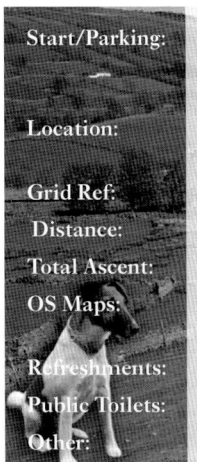

Start/Parking:	Middleton-in-Teesdale, in the car park by the memorial fountain. There is a second car park at the Working Men's Club near the bridge over Hudeshope Beck.
Location:	Middleton-in-Teesdale is situated 10 miles (16.1km) north-west of Barnard Castle on the B6277 Alston Road.
Grid Ref:	NY 948 254. Postcode: DL12 0SL.
Distance:	7½ miles (12.1km) circular. Allow 4 hrs walking time.
Total Ascent:	1083 feet (330m) Maximum Elevation: 1656 feet (505m).
OS Maps:	Explorer OL31 (1:25,000) or Landranger 91 (1:50,000) or Landranger 92 (1:50,000).
Refreshments:	Inns and cafes at Middleton-in-Teesdale.
Public Toilets:	Middleton-in-Teesdale, none en route.
Other:	Shops, Post Office, fish and chip shop, bus service, telephone.

Hardberry Hill and Hudeshope Beck

① *(GR: 948 254)* From the car park, turn left and follow the road towards Alston. Go past the Teesdale Hotel and cross the bridge over Hudeshope Beck.

② *(GR: 947 257)* Leave the main road and follow the road to Middle Side, which climbs steeply at first. Continue along the road climbing more gradually for just over two miles (3.2km) to the road junction near Stable Edge.

③ *(GR: 922 278)* Leave the road via a gate on the right *(SP Public Footpath)*. *(There are two gates with signposts close together but our route uses the second one)*. Follow a rough track uphill through two gates. Leave the track and continue climbing alongside the right wall. Go through a gate and stay with the wall, climbing to a stone step-stile.

④ *(GR: 928 283)* Go over the stile and continue climbing beside the wall. Near the wall corner bear right and cross another stone step-stile.

⑤ *(GR: 929 284)* Bear right and head roughly north-east to follow a sketchy path over the moor to a fence. Cross a wooden stile in the fence and descend to cross a stone step-stile in the wall.

⑥ *(GR: 937 288)* From the stile continue on roughly the same heading and descend to the Coldberry Lead Mine.

⑦ *(GR: 942 290)* Cross a wooden step-stile, turn right and follow a rough track alongside the fence to reach a minor road. Turn right, go through a gate and follow the road for about ten yards (9m).

⑧ *(GR: 944 286)* Leave the road via a stile on the left *(SP Public Footpath)*. Follow a clear path descending diagonally through the field. Cross a stone step-stile, continue descending over Club Gill Sike and go over another stone step-stile.

⑨ *(GR: 946 279)* Continue through three more fields and enter a woodland area via a ladder-stile and a wooden step-stile.

⑩ *(GR: 947 276)* Follow a clear track and begin a steep descent, cross a wooden step-stile at the bottom and a plank bridge. Bear right and follow a clear track alongside Hudeshope Beck to the Miners' Bridge and Skears kilns.

⑪ *(GR: 948 271)* Cross the bridge, turn right and follow a good tarmacked lane through the wood. *(There is a beckside path although it is not a public right-of-way)*.

⑫ *(GR: 948 259)* Turn right and continue descending to Middleton-in-Teesdale. Turn left at the road junction, go past the Teesdale Hotel and return to the car park.

LODGINGS – FIT FOR A KING!

Mine-shops, like this one at Coldberry, were built to house the lead miners between their working shifts. As many as forty miners lodged here in cramped conditions with little privacy. They elected a leader known as the 'king'. He held a regular court and the community will was expressed by a code of rules and the enforcement of discipline. Card-playing was strictly forbidden and defaulters had to pay a shilling into the shop fund which was used to buy cooking utensils and other amenities.

LUNEDALE and HARTER FELL

FROM MIDDLETON-IN-TEESDALE 8¼ MILES (13.3KM)

This scenic hill walk samples the delights of Lunedale. It begins with a gentle stroll through meadows and pastures, then a high level route reveals fine views of the valley and surrounding hills.

The star attraction of Middleton-in-Teesdale has to be its elaborate drinking fountain. It commemorates Robert Walton Bainbridge, who had been the superintendent of the London Lead Company. He was a fair but strict man who would not hesitate to fine a man found smoking in the street. The fountain was erected in 1877, at a cost of £35, using proceeds from his retirement collection. It was restored to its original elegance in 2000, at a cost of £12,000.

From the car park we follow the road over County Bridge, so called because the river Tees was originally the boundary between Durham and Yorkshire.

County Bridge was built on the remains of an earlier structure which collapsed shortly before its completion in 1811. Richard Attee, a local butcher, had often predicted the bridge's fate. Ironically, he was underneath the bridge, pointing out the defects to his wife when the structure gave way, causing fatal injuries to both of them. The present bridge dates from c.1813 and consists of a single arch with a span of about 80 feet (24m). Its original design incorporated circular holes, known as spandrel piercings, These reduced the weight of masonry which the arch had to support. The piercings were infilled c.1985 and the decorative circles are all that remain.

Our walk continues along the riverside to Step Ends Farm and then across the fields to Lonton where we join the Tees Railway Walk. This takes us over the Lune Viaduct, whose five impressive arches straddle the deep gorge of the river Lune. The Tees Valley Railway opened in 1868 and the original plan was to continue the line all the way to Alston to join with the South Tyne Valley Railway. However, apart from a short extension to a stone quarry at Holwick, construction ended at Middleton. The line closed in the 1960s.

From the viaduct we follow a quiet lane for a short distance, before favouring a path across the fields. After returning to the road the expanse of Grassholme Reservoir comes into view and within a few minutes we are enjoying the views from its shoreline.

Grassholme Reservoir occupies a beautiful setting surrounded by lush meadows that are intersected by dry stone walls and dotted with traditional stone barns. It was completed in 1915 and covers an area of 140 acres (57ha), reaching a depth of 120 feet (37m) at the dam. The visitor centre has a hands-on exhibition explaining the function and history of the reservoirs.

To the west of the lake, above Grassholme Bridge, a nature reserve provides essential refuge for many species of wild birds. In the breeding season a colony of about 900 pairs of black-headed gulls nest on the wetlands near the main inflow. There is also a colony of jackdaws nesting in disused rabbit burrows near the bridge. The jackdaw is notorious for its thieving habits, often taking shining objects, and in Thomas Ingoldsby's tale *The Jackdaw of Rheims*, the bird is cursed for stealing the cardinal's ring. Other common visitors include lapwing, oystercatcher, snipe, wigeon and teal. Mammals living in the reserve include rabbit, water vole and short-tailed vole, while the shallows at the water's edge encourage the common toad to breed.

Leaving the reservoir behind we follow the road to Grassholme Farm, where the Pennine Way is joined. This leads uphill to the Brough-Middleton road, a lane opposite takes us past the remote Wythes Hill Farm and onto rough pasture. There are superb views of Lunedale, stretching the full length of Grassholme Reservoir. We continue over the shoulder of Harter Fell and Middleton suddenly appears below, like an oasis in the desert.

The distinctive clump of Scots pines to the right marks the site of a large tumulus called Kirkcarrion. Excavations in 1804 yielded a stone-lined grave containing a cinery urn with fragments of bone and ashes inside it, suggesting it was a Bronze Age burial site. However, the remains are reputed, by some scholars, to be those of a Brigantian prince called Caryn. Hence the name, Kirkcarrion, meaning Caryn's Church. Caryn's unsettled spirit stalks the fells, no doubt lamenting the disturbance of his Celtic tomb.

As we descend to Middleton a glorious panorama of the valley is revealed, enticing us to explore it more intimately, but, today our thirst is fulfilled, or it soon will be!

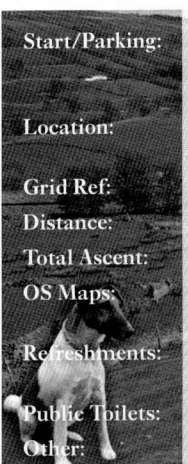

Start/Parking:	Middleton-in-Teesdale, in the car park by the memorial fountain. There is a second car park at the Working Men's Club near the bridge over Hudeshope Beck.
Location:	Middleton-in-Teesdale is situated 10 miles (16.1km) north-west of Barnard Castle on the B6277 Alston Road.
Grid Ref:	NY 948 254. Postcode: DL12 0SL.
Distance:	8¼ miles (13.3km) circular. Allow 4 hrs walking time.
Total Ascent:	951 feet (290m) Maximum Elevation: 1444 feet (440m).
OS Maps:	Explorer OL31 (1:25,000), Landranger 91 (1:50,000) or Landranger 92 (1:50,000).
Refreshments:	Inns and cafes at Middleton-in-Teesdale and a cafe at Grassholme Reservoir.
Public Toilets:	Middleton-in-Teesdale and Grassholme Reservoir.
Other:	Shops, Post Office, fish and chip shop, bus service, telephone.

Lunedale and Harter Fell

① *(GR: 948 254)* From the car park entrance turn left. At the road junction turn left *(SP Brough)* and follow the road down to cross the bridge over the river Tees.

② *(GR: 946 252)* Go through a gate on the left and down the steps *(SP Public Footpath)*. Continue along the riverbank and join a tarmacked farm road. Follow the road past the farm where a rougher track leads to a stone step-stile.

③ *(GR: 950 248)* Cross the stile and bear half right climbing up to go through a gap-stile. Continue diagonally across the next two fields returning to the road.

④ *(GR: 953 245)* Turn right and follow the road to the first bend. Leave the road along an enclosed track on the left *(sign Tees Railway Walk)*. Follow this track for about half a mile (800m) and cross the Lune viaduct.

⑤ *(GR: 959 240)* Turn right and follow the road to Westfield House. Leave the road via a gate on the left *(SP Public Footpath)*. Continue along rough farm track climbing gradually to 'The Acres'. Cross a wooden step-stile, follow the left wall past a barn and then go through a gap-stile.

⑥ *(GR: 958 236)* Bear right and descend to stile in bottom right of the field. Go through the stile, bear left and go through another stile by a gate. Follow the right wall, climbing steeply, crossing two fences.

⑦ *(GR: 956 231)* Go through a stile in the right wall, bear half left and continue climbing towards the far top corner of the field. Go through a gap-stile onto the road near a T-junction. Turn right and follow the road to Grassholme Reservoir.

⑧ *(GR: 948 225)* Leave the main road and follow the road down to the right, take the second left turn and pass below the information centre/cafe, continue through the car park. Go through a gate and follow a clear path around the reservoir.

⑨ *(GR: 930 215)* Turn right and follow the road across the bridge. Follow the road uphill to Grassholme Farm.

⑩ *(GR: 926 216)* Leave the road via a gate on the right *(SP Pennine Way)*. Go straight across the farmyard and through a gate. Bear half right and after a short descent climb steeply to go through a gap-stile. Continue climbing towards the barn on the left. Go through a stile, descend to cross some stepping stones. Climb back up and continue through three more stiles to reach the Brough-Middleton road.

⑪ *(GR: 924 225)* Cross the road and follow a tarmacked farm lane uphill to Wythes Hill Farm. Pass to the left of the farm and continue climbing along a rough enclosed track. Follow this round to the right and descend to cross a stream.

⑫ *(GR: 922 229)* Go through a gate and begin climbing again. Head towards the top right corner and go through a stile. Continue climbing, diagonally left, across the next two pastures.

⑬ *(GR: 924 233)* Go through the stile, bear right and follow a rough track to a gate/stile. Keep in line with the right wall through the next two pastures. Continue along a broad green path passing through a gate and then bear left to another gate.

⑭ *(GR: 930 235)* Go through the gate and continue along the track, climbing more gradually. Go through a gate, follow the left boundary and go through a broken wall. Go past a cairn and continue towards the far right corner of the field. Go through the gate and begin the long descent to Middleton-in-Teesdale.

⑮ *(GR: 941 243)* Cross a wooden step-stile, *(doggie friendly)*, continue descending and go through a gate in the bottom right of the field.

⑯ *(GR: 946 248)* Keep close to the right wall, descend to the right of the farm and go through a gate leading onto the road. Turn right and at the road junction turn left. Follow the road downhill past the Auction Mart and return to the car park.

BALDERSDALE and COTHERSTONE MOOR

from Hury Reservoir 7½ miles (12.1km)

Starting from Hury Reservoir, this walk explores the beautiful valley of Baldersdale. Once again the views are stunning and there is a good variety of habitats for wild flowers and birds. All of this can be enjoyed with a minimum of effort.

Baldersdale was the birthplace of Hannah Hauxwell, a truly remarkable lady who was catapulted to fame in Yorkshire Television's award-winning documentary *Too Long a Winter* and its sequel *A Winter Too Many*, Hannah lived alone in a remote farmhouse above Blackton Reservoir with neither gas nor electricity and all of her water had to be carried from a nearby stream. In a good year she made a profit of £280 working long hours in all weather conditions. In 1988 Hannah left the toil of farmwork behind and moved to a cottage at Cotherstone. She had rarely travelled outside the boundaries of her own county, but this was soon remedied with trips to Europe and the USA for further documentaries *An Innocent Abroad* and *Hannah USA*.

Durham Wildlife Trust acquired the fields at Hannah's Meadow and they are still farmed by traditional methods without using artificial fertilisers. The meadows are best seen in June and July when they are rich in flowering plants including globeflower, wood anemone and adder's tongue fern. The old barn in the top meadow is now used as a visitor centre with displays describing Hannah's life.

Like neighbouring Lunedale, Baldersdale has been pressed into service by the water authorities and its river, the Balder, is tamed by three large reservoirs, Balderhead, Blackton and Hury which was the first of Teesdale's reservoirs. Hury was completed in 1894 and covers an area of 125 acres (50.6ha) with a maximum depth of 90 feet (27m). An underground pipeline connects Hury to Grassholme

Reservoir in Lunedale. This can transfer 50 million gallons (227 million litres) of water each day between the two valleys.

After crossing the dam we follow the road for a short distance and then continue through the fields above the river Balder. During the last survey we came across a riggwelted sheep along this section of the walk. When a sheep is on its back and unable to get up without assistance, the local dales dialect says it's 'rigged' or 'riggwelted' from the Old Norse; *rygg*-back and *velte*-to overturn. My friend went to assist the sheep, gently rocking it back and forth until it could get up onto its feet. However, the sheep was not so gentle and kicked out at its willing helper!

Further on we pass the magnificent nine-arched Balder Viaduct which spans the deep, wooded ravine of the river Balder. The viaduct was part of the Tees Valley Railway line and it is a monument to the skills of the Victorian engineers who constructed the railway in 1868. The line closed in 1965 and it now constitutes the Tees Valley Railway Walk, a leisurely six mile (10km) ramble, between Lonton and Lartington.

Our route leads us to Doe Park where we descend to the road at Balder Bridge and continue into Cotherstone, one of the most beautiful villages in Teesdale. The village grew as a farming community from Anglo-Saxon times. When the Tees Valley Railway opened Cotherstone became a popular holiday resort and is still favoured by visitors, with two inns serving excellent fayre. The local Cotherstone cheese, for which the village is most famous, is probably a descendant of Wensleydale. It was originally made with ewes' milk and would have tasted quite different from today's cheese which uses cows' milk.

Leaving Cotherstone our walk continues through the meadows and after returning to the road we follow it uphill to the Butter Stone. This large solitary boulder was used during the plague of 1663-65, when villages isolated themselves in the hope that they would be able to avoid infection. The Butter Stone was an appointed place of exchange; farm produce was left near the stone; payment was placed in the groove in the top of the stone which was filled with vinegar. This was thought to have had the necessary disinfecting properties.

As we progress across Cotherstone Moor a wonderful panorama of Baldersdale gradually unfolds before us. The flat-topped outcrop of Goldsbrough stands out prominently on the horizon to the left. The moor sustains a large variety of breeding birds including red grouse, curlew, snipe, dunlin, lapwing, redshank and moorland raptors such as merlin and short-eared owl.

Descending from the moor we arrive at the tiny hamlet of Briscoe, which is worthy of a closer look before returning to Hury.

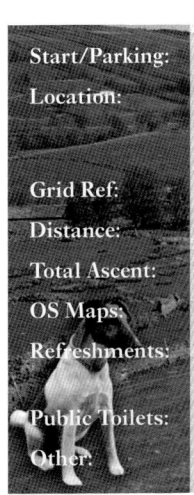

Start/Parking:	Hury Reservoir.
Location:	Hury Reservoir is located 2½ miles (4km) west of Cotherstone. Cotherstone is situated 4 miles (6.4km) north-west of Barnard Castle on the B6277 Alston Road.
Grid Ref:	NY 966 192. Postcode: DL12 9UL.
Distance:	7½ miles (12.1km) circular. Allow 4 hrs walking time.
Total Ascent:	492 feet (150m) Maximum Elevation: 919 feet (280m).
OS Maps:	Explorer OL31 (1:25,000) or Landranger 92 (1:50,000).
Refreshments:	The Fox and Hounds Inn, the Red Lion Hotel and the Mill Tea Room at Cotherstone.
Public Toilets:	Hury Reservoir, none en route.
Other:	Post Office, telephone, bus service.

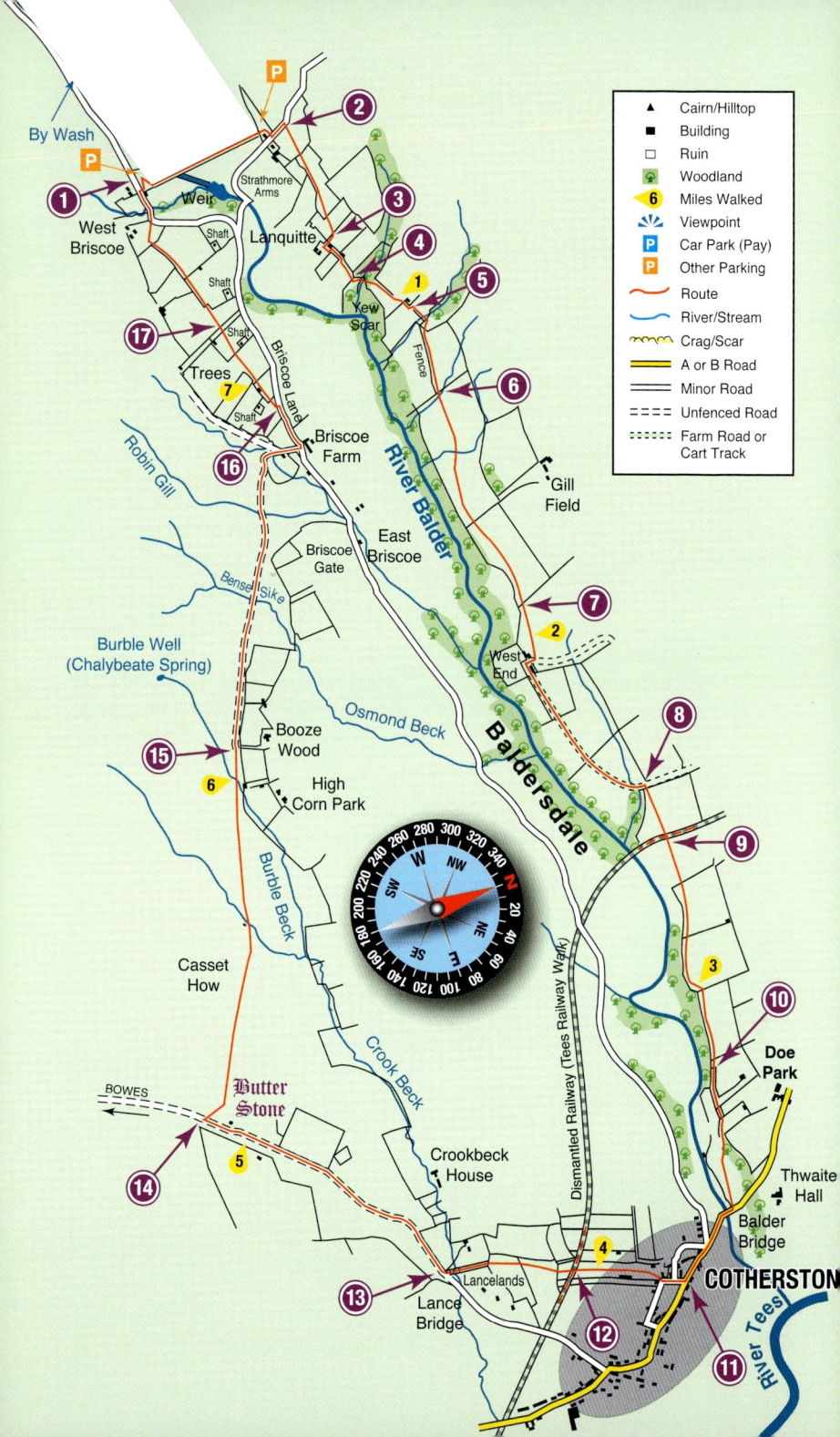

Baldersdale and Cotherstone Moor

1 *(GR: 966 192)* Leave the car park via a gate opposite the entrance. Follow a grassy track across the dam and go through a gate at the end. Turn right and go through a gate onto the road. Turn left and follow the road uphill for about 150 yards (137m).

2 *(GR: 966 198)* Leave the road via a stile *(SP Public Footpath)*. Go straight across the field and go through a gate. Continue across two more fields to a gate.

3 *(GR: 971 198)* Go through the gate and turn right. Descend beside the wall and go through a gate. Turn left to pass in front of the barn. Continue along an enclosed track and then follow the left boundary through an open gateway.

4 *(GR: 972 199)* Descend to the left and cross the stream via a footbridge. Climb to the wall at the top of the field. Turn right and follow the wall to its demise. Now continue to pass through a gate below a barn.

5 *(GR: 974 200)* Go through a gap in the wall, turn right and follow the wall to cross a stream. A few yards upstream go over a waymarked ladder-stile and bear right climbing over a small ridge. Descend via a broken wall to a fence and turn left. Continue along the fence to a gate.

6 *(GR: 977 200)* Go through the gate and continue across a large pasture, go through a gap-stile and follow a clear path towards the far right corner of the pasture.

7 *(GR: 986 201)* Go through the gate and head towards the farm buildings. After passing the barn go through a gate on the right and pass between the barns. Turn left and follow a rough farm road through three fields, descending slightly.

8 *(GR: 994 203)* After crossing a small stream leave the rough farm road via a gate on the right *(yellow waymark)*. Continue through the field, go through a kissing gate and descend some steps. Cross the former Tees Valley railway line, climb back up and go through another kissing gate.

9 *(GR: 995 203)* Head straight across the field, go through a gate and follow the right fence through three more gates.

10 *(GR: 004 202)* Continue along the right boundary, go through a gate and follow an enclosed path via another gate and stile passing the caravan park. Keep to the right and descend to the road at Balder Bridge. Turn right and follow the road uphill into Cotherstone.

11 *(GR: 011 198)* Go past the Fox and Hounds public house, turn right and follow a narrow tarmacked lane. At a left bend, leave the lane via a gate on the right *(SP Public Footpath)*. Bear left towards the middle of the field and then climb to a stile in the top fence.

12 *(GR: 009 194)* Cross two ladder-stiles *(crossing the former railway line)*. Continue straight across the field and go through a gap stile. Bear right slightly and climb up to go through a stile beside a gate. Continue over a step-stile and follow a fenced path over another step-stile, a slab bridge and a gap-stile to reach the main road.

13 *(GR: 008 190)* Turn right and follow the road uphill for about ¾ miles (1.2km) passing the Butter Stone.

14 *(GR: 999 183)* Leave the road *(SP Public Bridleway)* and follow a clear path across the open moorland to Booze Wood.

15 *(GR: 987 189)* Join a tarmacked lane and follow it to Briscoe Farm, crossing a cattle grid. At the road junction turn left and continue along the road for 150 yards (137m).

16 *(GR: 976 194)* Leave the road via a stile on the left *(SP Public Footpath)* Bear right and go through a gap-stile. Continue via three more gap-stiles and a step-stile.

17 *(GR: 972 193)* Head straight across the field and go through a gate. Continue with the left wall through two more gates. Descend to the right and go through a gate leading onto the main road. Turn left and follow the road back to the car park at Hury.

EGGLESTON BRIDGE and ROMALDKIRK

FROM COTHERSTONE 6 MILES (9.6KM)

Fairy cupboards, a finishing school for girls and a 'beck of beer' can all be found during this scenic walk. There are a couple of short climbs but nothing too strenuous.

Cotherstone is an elegant village situated near the confluence of the rivers Balder and Tees. It is a long straggling settlement with a small green at each end, giving the impression that it may have started out as two independent communities. Standing near the centre of the village is St Cuthbert's Church which was built in 1881. It has a peal of six bells which were hung for full-circle ringing. However, the positioning of the clock mechanism, which takes pride of place in the centre of the ringing room, must cause a degree of obstruction to some of the bell-ringers.

The manor of Cotherstone was given to the Fitzhughs, of Ravensworth, soon after the Norman Conquest. In 1201 they were granted a royal licence to convert their manor house on Hallgarth Hill into a castle. Tradition has it that the castle was burnt down by the Scots during one of their many raids, and fragments of burnt timber which have been excavated on the site appear to support this story. The remains include a small section of one wall belonging to the keep, an earth mound and traces of a probable fishpond.

Leaving Cotherstone we cross the rivers Balder and Tees and continue uphill to Percy Myre Rock. From the summit of this cliff there are wonderful views of Teesdale; to the left, the spire of St Cuthbert's Church rises high above the rooftops of Cotherstone; across the valley, the distant hills of Goldsborough and Shackleborough stand out; and below, the Tees winds its way through the deep wooded ravine. According to legend, Lord Percy, the last of the Fitzhughs, fell to his death over this cliff. Despite the warnings of a local wise woman, he went out hunting. He was in close pursuit of a stag, near Percy Myre Rock, when his tired horse stumbled and fell into the ravine along with its rider.

After returning to the main route we continue via East Barnley Farm to Great Wood where we descend the Jubilee Steps. These were constructed in 1985 to mark the golden jubilee of the Ramblers' Association, hence their name.

Our route continues to Eggleston Bridge where we cross the river Tees once more. Eggleston Bridge dates from the fifteenth century and once incorporated a chantry chapel on the Yorkshire side. However, no trace of this is now visible. Some rebuilding was undertaken in 1653. In 1982 it was reinforced with a concrete saddle and the parapets were rebuilt, otherwise this graceful two-arched structure has remained relatively unchanged for six centuries.

From the bridge we continue through lush meadows to Romaldkirk and at the first stile look back for a view of Eggleston Hall. This classical Georgian country house has an impressive mixture of natural beauty and architectural style. The hall housed one of Britain's top finishing schools for twenty years, offering cookery and flower arranging courses. It's doors were re-opened for the ITV series *Ladette to Lady*. The series followed the progress of ten young women, who usually behaved in a crude and drunken manner. They received tutoring in the necessary skills in an attempt to become ladies.

Approaching Romaldkirk we cross the quaintly named Beer Beck, but with two pubs in the village it would be more sensible to quench your thirst at one of those instead! Romaldkirk is a peaceful and unspoiled village appearing much as it did in the eighteenth century. It has three spacious greens edged by stone-built houses and the magnificent twelfth-century St Romald's Church, also known as the Cathedral of the Dales. The finishing touches are provided by the stocks, water pumps and the village pound – where straying livestock was held until a fine was paid by the offender.

We leave the village along a delightful tree-shaded lane and then descend through lush meadows to the river Tees. Our path leads to the 'fairy cupboards' – small recesses that have been scoured out of the rock by the action of water erosion. These cupboards have a curious formation and appear as though they are supported by rounded pillars. The perfect place for fairies to store their possessions!

Climbing back up from the river we pass Woden Croft, reputed to have been one of those infamous boarding schools described by Charles Dickens in *Nicholas Nickleby*. From here we descend to the river one more time and follow it back to Cotherstone.

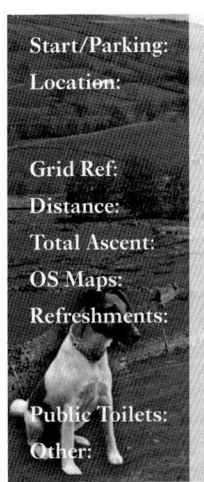

Start/Parking:	Small car park at the Hagg in Cotherstone.
Location:	Cotherstone is situated 4 miles (6.4km) north-west of Barnard Castle on the B6277 Alston Road. The Hagg is located down a narrow lane opposite the Fox and Hounds.
Grid Ref:	NY 011 200. Postcode: DL12 9QJ.
Distance:	6 miles (9.6km) circular. Allow 3½ hrs walking time.
Total Ascent:	492 feet (150m) Maximum Elevation: 820 feet (250m).
OS Maps:	Explorer OL31 (1:25,000) or Landranger 92 (1:50,000).
Refreshments:	The Fox and Hounds Inn, the Red Lion Hotel and the Mill Tea Room at Cotherstone.
	The Kirk Inn and the Rose and the Crown Hotel at Romaldkirk.
Public Toilets:	None en route, nearest Barnard Castle.
Other:	Post Office, telephone, bus service.

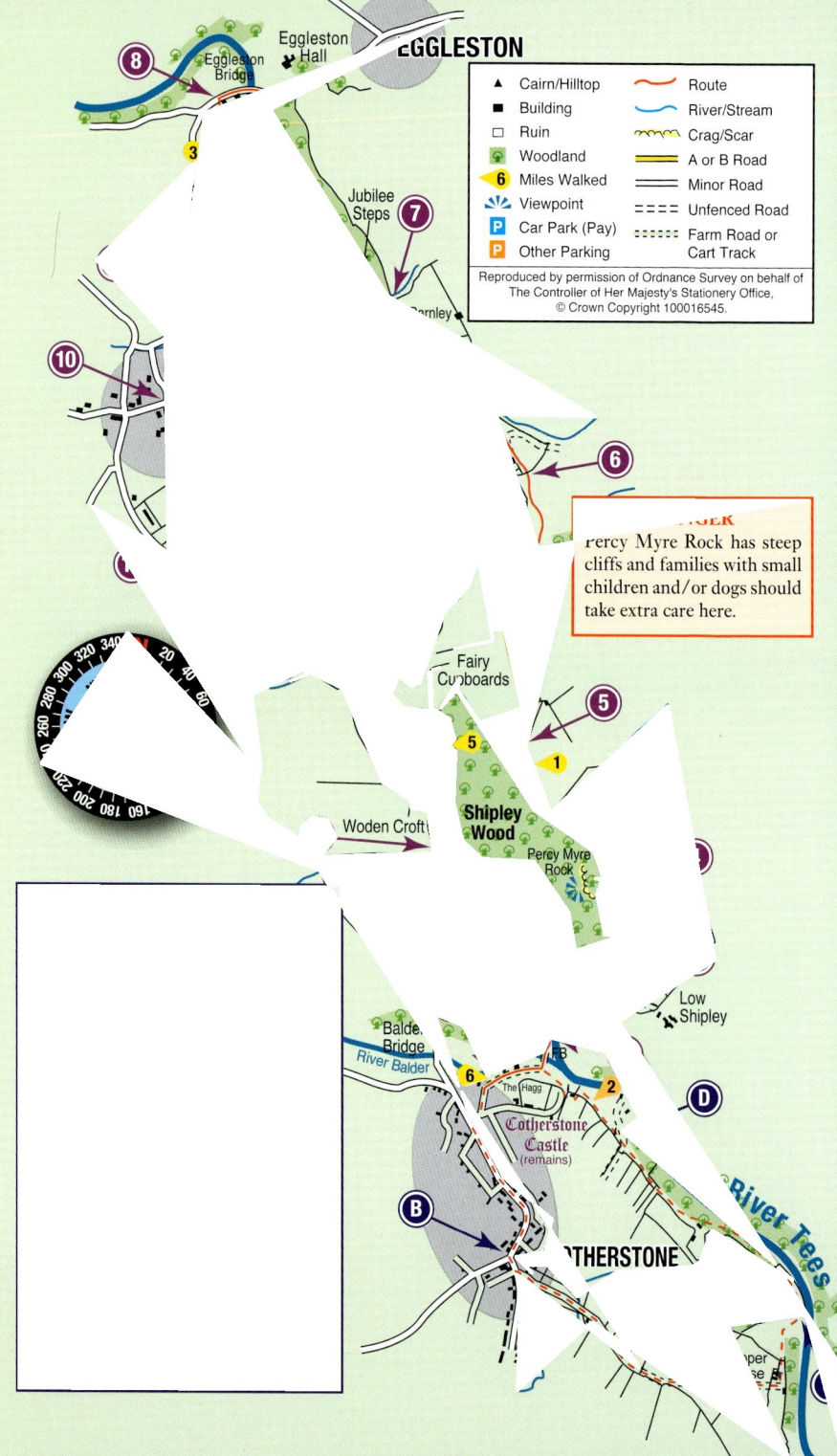

Eggleston Bridge and Romaldkirk

(1) *(GR: 011 200)* From the parking place follow the lane down to the river Tees. Turn left and cross a footbridge over the river Balder. Continue along a good track to Cotherstone's footbridge over the Tees.

(2) *(GR: 013 202)* Cross the footbridge and continue straight ahead for about ten yards (9m) bear left *(SP Teesdale Way)*. Join a good track climbing steeply and go through a gate leading into a caravan park. Continue straight across the park to a waymark post between the caravans.

(3) *(GR: 015 204)* Climb up a steep track leading through the gorse and cross a wooden step-stile. Bear left slightly and head towards a stone step-stile leading into the wood. Follow the right wall round and leave the wood via another stone step-stile.

(4) *(GR: 015 206)* Turn left, cross a small stream and follow the waymarks through the field. Percy Myre Rock is reached via a stone step stile in the left wall. Retrace your steps, turn left and follow the left boundary, crossing two more stone step-stiles. Continue on a good track along the right fence.

(5) *(GR: 010 212)* Leave the track and head towards a stone step-stile in the wall. Cross the stile and descend to cross a wooden step-stile in the fence opposite. Climb back up and cross a stone step-stile, cross a stream and follow a clear path to East Barnley.

(6) *(GR: 009 221)* Go through the gate and pass behind the farm buildings, cross the farm road and descend to cross a stile in the bottom left of the field. Continue descending to the far left corner and cross a stone step-stile. Now follow the left boundary through the field.

(7) *(GR: 003 226)* Pass through a gate into the wood, follow a clear path which descends to the Jubilee Steps and onto a tarmacked lane. Turn right and follow the lane to the main road near Eggleston Bridge. Turn left and follow the road across the bridge.

(8) *(GR: 996 232)* Leave the road via a stone step-stile on the left *(SP Teesdale Way)*. Follow a clear path climbing to the right and cross a wooden step-stile in the top left corner. Turn left and follow the field boundary round to a stone step-stile.

(9) *(GR: 997 226)* Go through the stile and descend towards the wood at the bottom of the field. Cross a stone step-stile and follow the right fence round to cross the stream *(this is called Beer Beck)*. Continue along an enclosed track leading into Romaldkirk. Turn right and continue to the main road.

(10) *(GR: 996 221)* Turn left and follow the road passing to the left of the Kirk Inn. Continue along a private drive *(SP Teesdale Way)* and go past the houses to join an enclosed track. Follow this to its end, where we reach two gates.

(11) *(GR: 998 217)* Go through the left gate *(waymark Teesdale Way)*. Bear left and follow a clear path which descends through two gates to reach the derelict farmhouse at Low Garth. Cross the stile and turn left to pass in front of the farm. Descend to cross a wooden step-stile *(waymark Teesdale Way)* leading into the wood.

(12) *(GR: 005 215)* Follow a clear path descending to the river Tees and continue downstream. After scrambling over some boulders climb back up away from the river and go through a gate at the top. Turn left and follow the left boundary through three gates to Woden Croft. Continue in front of the farmhouse and go through another gate.

(13) *(GR: 008 207)* Turn left and follow the left boundary, go through two gates passing a walled orchard. Continue descending gradually and cross a wooden step-stile.

(14) *(GR: 012 206)* Turn right and cross the stream via the stepping stones. Climb up some steps and follow the right fence to a wooden step-stile, cross this and bear left across the meadow. Cross another wooden step-stile *(doggie friendly - I wish that there were more like this)*. Follow a good path which leads back to Cotherstone's footbridge. Now follow the outward route back to the parking place.

LARTINGTON and DEEPDALE

FROM BARNARD CASTLE 6¾ MILES (10.9KM)

This route has a delightful blend of woodland and river scenery. We visit the cosy little village of Lartington and explore the sylvan valley of Deepdale Beck where a wide range of flora and fauna can be enjoyed.

Barnard Castle, or 'Barney' as it is more affectionately known, is an ancient market town. It grew up in the shadow of Bernard de Balliol's magnificent fortress, after which it is named. The castle dates from 1125 when the original timber structure was rebuilt in stone. It stands 80 feet (24m) above the river Tees and uses the natural defence of almost sheer cliffs on the west and south sides. The remains include the Great Hall and a large circular keep – the Round Tower, also known as the Balliol Tower.

In 1569, during the Rising of the North, a Catholic plot to depose Queen Elizabeth I and replace her with Mary, Queen of Scots emerged and Barnard Castle was besieged by five thousand rebels. Sir George Bowes, the governor of the castle, held out for eleven days before he was forced to surrender after the water supply had been cut off. However, this delay gave sufficient time for the royal forces to march north and suppress the rebellion.

The town's best-known landmark, after the castle, is its large octagonal market cross which dominates the market place. This was built in 1747 and has been used for a variety of purposes since that time; on market days dairy produce and eggs were sold here, which led to the building being called the Butter Cross or Butter Market. It has also served as the Town Hall, Court House and at one time it was used as the town jail. The weather-vane on top of the cross is marked by two bullet holes, said to have been made in 1804 by a gamekeeper and a volunteer soldier, during a contest to prove who was the better marksman.

34

From the car park our route passes the castle and descends along a tree-shaded lane to the Tees Aqueduct. This was constructed in 1893 to convey water from the reservoirs in Baldersdale to the towns and industries on Teesside. The aqueduct, known locally as the Water Bridge, provides a safe crossing of the river and has a fine view of the castle.

After crossing the river we follow the Teesdale Way to the remains of the Tees Viaduct. This was built in 1861 to carry the railway to Kirby Stephen and Middleton-in-Teesdale. The viaduct had six tall piers, four of which stood in the river. The line closed in 1965 and the viaduct was demolished in 1972. Plans were put forward, in 2002, to erect a rope suspension bridge between the two remaining piers. If this ever came to fruition, it would be the world's longest rope suspension bridge at a distance of 600 feet (183m).

Our walk continues through the fields to Lartington Hall. Built in 1635 during the reign of Charles I, Lartington Hall was the ancestral home of the Maires family. They were one of the North's wealthiest Catholic families, whose ancestry has been traced to the twelfth-century Lords of Appleby. The hall served as a Red Cross convalescent home during the war and after extensive restoration it became a hotel. The restored gardens were originally laid out by architect Joseph Hansom, most famous for introducing the Hansom cab.

Lartington has many fine cottages, most of which line the road facing the former village green. This area has been landscaped at some time and is planted with Giant Wellingtonia trees. There are also traces of ornamental ponds and waterfalls.

Leaving the village we pass the Lartington Aqueduct and then continue into the sylvan valley of Deepdale. The aqueduct was built in 1863 to take the beck over a railway cutting, through which the South Durham and Lancashire Union Railway ran. We also pass the site of the Deepdale Viaduct, opened in 1861, to carry the railway on to Tebay. This was 740 feet (225m) in length with eleven spans across the river and it stood 161 feet (49m) above Deepdale Beck.

Deepdale contains some of the richest deciduous woodland in Upper Teesdale and is a haven for birds and wild flowers. Great spotted woodpecker, robin, tree creeper and grey wagtail are often seen and, with patience, kingfisher. You may also spot the brown argus and dark green fritillary butterflies. Our path leads us back to the main road.

Now we follow the road into Barnard Castle via County Bridge, another bridge so named because the river Tees was the former border of Yorkshire and the Palatinate of Durham. From the bridge we continue up through the town passing the Butter Cross and return to our parking place.

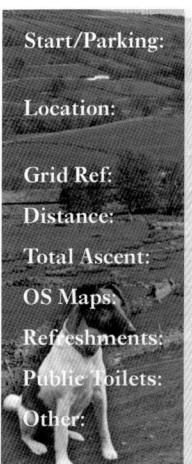

Start/Parking:	Large car park, adjacent to Morrisons Supermarket, just off Galgate, at Barnard Castle.
Location:	Barnard Castle is situated 17 miles (27km) west of Darlington on the A67 Darlington road.
Grid Ref:	NZ 051 166. Postcode: DL12 8JJ.
Distance:	6¾ miles (10.9km) circular. Allow 3 hrs walking time.
Total Ascent:	836 feet (255m) Maximum Elevation: 740 feet (226m).
OS Maps:	Explorer OL31 (1:25,000) or Landranger 92 (1:50,000).
Refreshments:	Inns, cafes and restaurants in Barnard Castle.
Public Toilets:	Barnard Castle, none en route.
Other:	Post Office, banks, supermarkets, shops, fish and chip shop, bus service, telephone, the Bowes Museum.

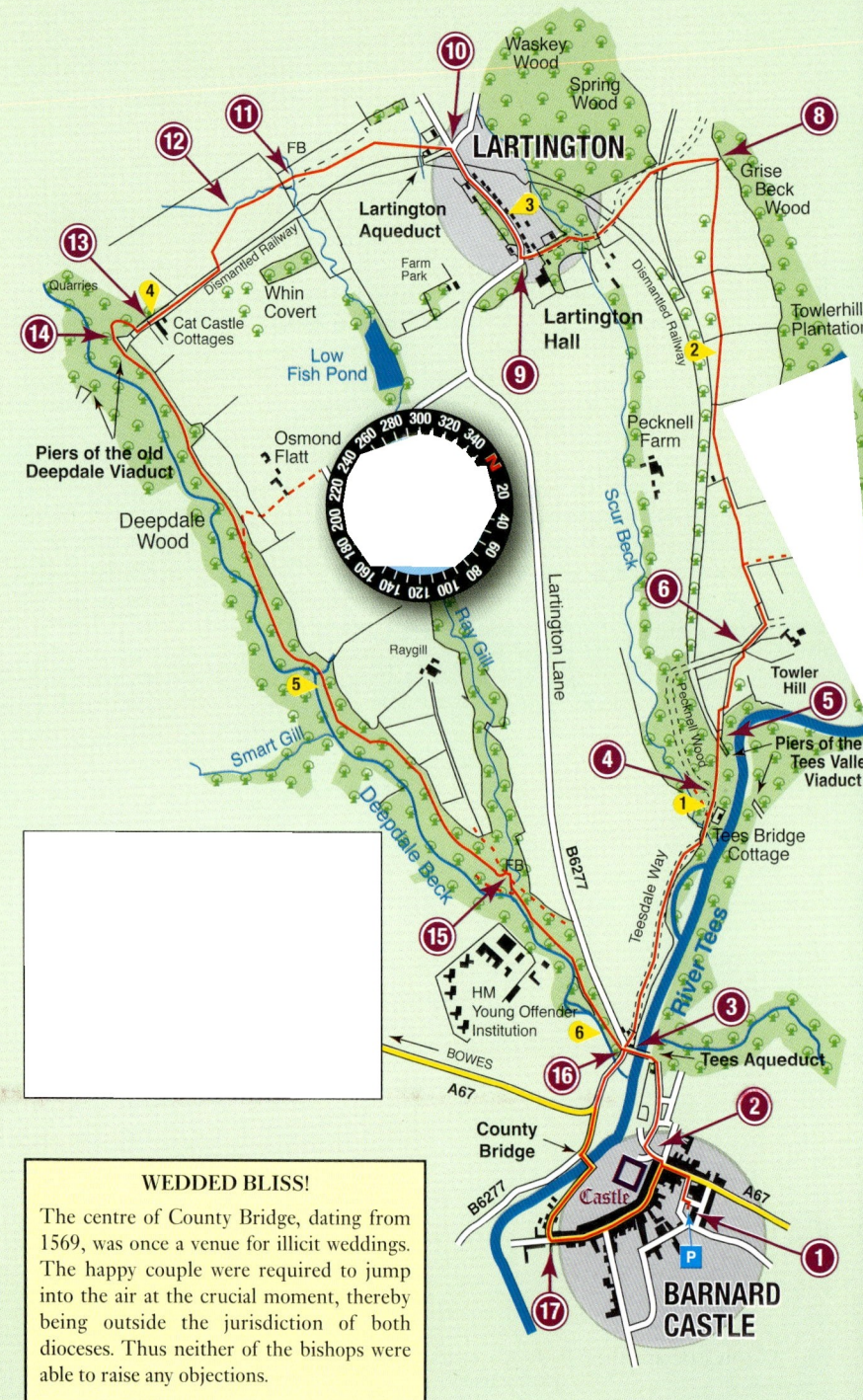

WEDDED BLISS!

The centre of County Bridge, dating from 1569, was once a venue for illicit weddings. The happy couple were required to jump into the air at the crucial moment, thereby being outside the jurisdiction of both dioceses. Thus neither of the bishops were able to raise any objections.

Lartington and Deepdale

① *(GR: 051 166)* From the car park return to the main road, turn left and locate the pedestrian traffic signals. Cross the road and then follow the road towards the castle. Take the right fork, *(unless you wish to visit the castle first)*.

② *(GR: 049 166)* Turn right *(SP Cotherstone)*, and follow the lane past the child's play area and crazy golf. Continue along the lane descending to the river Tees and a footbridge *(the Tees Aqueduct)*. Cross the bridge and continue to the main road.

③ *(GR: 045 167)* Turn right and after about ten yards (9m) leave the road along a private drive *(SP The Teesdale Way)*. Go through two gates and follow a tarmacked lane, then go through a gate by a cattle grid and continue past Tees Bridge Cottage.

④ *(GR: 040 174)* About thirty yards (27m) past the cottage leave the lane to follow a narrow forest path on the right *(waymark the Teesdale Way)*. Continue over a waymarked stile and climb up through the wood to the remains of the Tees Railway Viaduct.

⑤ *(GR: 038 175)* From the top of the steps head right and go over a step-stile in the corner. Follow the right hedge and cross a step-stile on the right. Turn left and follow the left boundary through the field. Go over a step-stile and join a tarmacked lane.

⑥ *(GR: 036 178)* Turn right and follow the lane for about 100 yards (91m). Turn left *(waymark the Teesdale Way)* and follow a fenced track through a gate. Follow the right fence to its corner and then continue straight ahead towards some tall oak trees. Continue through a gate and bear left towards the far left corner of the field.

⑦ *(GR: 028 180)* Go through the gate and bear right towards a gate beside a tall oak tree. Go through the gate and follow the line of a former hedgerow across the field. Continue through an opening in the fence and head towards the far right corner of the field.

⑧ *(GR: 021 185)* Go through the gate and turn left. Follow the left fence and cross the former railway line via a gate and a bridge. Now head directly across the field towards the old railway bridge. Pass under the bridge and continue along a rough farm track. Go through a gate and turn right onto a tarmacked lane, follow this past Lartington Hall to the main road.

⑨ *(GR: 021 177)* Turn right and follow the main road through the village to a T-Junction on a right-hand bend.

⑩ *(GR: 016 176)* Leave the road via a gate on the left *(SP Public Footpath)*. Head diagonally across the field and cross Lartington Beck. Continue in the same direction climbing up to the hedge boundary. Turn left and follow the hedge, descending to a footbridge.

⑪ *(GR: 014 171)* Cross the footbridge and go through the gate opposite. Now continue straight ahead, cross a small beck and follow it uphill to a bridge.

⑫ *(GR: 014 169)* Bear left here and head towards a gate in the left boundary. Turn right and follow the lane *(dismantled railway)*. Pass an old signal box and the Cat Castle Cottages. Continue to the end of the lane.

⑬ *(GR: 016 165)* Cross the stile at the end of the lane. Follow a narrow path along the left boundary and after about ten yards (9m) bear right and descend to a waymark.

⑭ *(GR: 015 164)* Turn left and follow a waymarked path leading through Deepdale Wood. *(About ten yards (9m) along the track are the remains of the Deepdale Viaduct)*. The track meanders up and down, and the vegetation can be quite dense in places.

⑮ *(GR: 038 166)* Turn right and cross a footbridge. Turn right again and continue down to join a broad track. Turn left and follow this track back to the main road.

⑯ *(GR: 045 167)* Cross the road, turn right and follow the road to County Bridge. Cross the bridge, turn right and continue along the road into Barnard Castle.

⑰ *(GR: 050 162)* Turn left and follow the road uphill, keep left past the Butter Cross. Continue through the market place and at the road junction near the castle turn right. Now follow the outward route back to the car park.

37

BOWES, DEEPDALE and GOD'S BRIDGE

FROM BOWES 8 MILES (12.9KM)

Charles Dickens, a medieval castle and God's Bridge each play their part in this memorable walk. It begins with a march into Deepdale with beautiful views all the way. On the return there are many opportunities to study the wide variety of flora and fauna.

Bowes, situated above the river Greta, derives its name from the Old Norse *bogr* meaning 'bow' and signifies 'the river-bends'. The village also occupies a strategic position at the entrance to the bleak and isolated Stainmore Pass which has been an important trading route across the Northern Pennines for thousands of years. Finds of a flat bronze axe and a stone battleaxe at Bowes, suggest that the route was in use during the Early Bronze Age *c.*1500 BC. Once established, the route grew in importance and it became a vital military link during the Roman occupation of Britain AD 43 to AD 410.

Bowes Castle, founded by Conan the Little, Earl of Richmond *c.*1136, was completed for Henry II by Richard the Engineer between 1171-87. The castle was more a garrisoned outpost and watch-tower than a residential castle for it was a solitary keep that stood without the protection of curtain walls. A rectangular ditch enclosure was its only outer defence. It was besieged by marauding Scots in 1174 and again, by Robert the Bruce, in 1322 after which the castle fell into ruin.

The castle stands in the north-west corner of the Roman fort, Lavatrae, built in the first century AD to guard the eastern approaches to the Stainmore Pass. It covered an area of four acres (1.6ha) and was occupied by a legion famous for its Spanish horses. This was one of the last Roman outposts on the northern frontier to be abandoned.

Charles Dickens came to Bowes in 1838 to find out if the disturbing stories about the

Yorkshire Schools were true. He had been told of boy-farms where unwanted sons and nephews were sent and held like prisoners, in unhygienic conditions where they were often bullied and almost starved. Dickens visited William Shaw's Academy which became Dotheboys Hall in Nicholas Nickleby and Shaw was immortalised as Wackford Squeers. The public outcry created by Dickens' novel forced the closure of many such schools. Shaws Academy closed in 1842.

After passing Dotheboys we continue over the busy A66 bypass. As height is gained look back for a view of Bowes, dominated by the castle, with wild moorland behind. Ahead, over the crest of the hill, the views extend across Deepdale to the higher Teesdale fells. The road ends at West Stony Keld and we continue across open moorland to Pasture End.

Britain has 75 per cent of the entire world's open heather moorland, most of this being managed for use as grouse moor. Controlled burning of the heather is carried out and this encourages the growth of young shoots on which the grouse feed. It also helps to retain the habitats of other moorland birds, including curlew, dunlin, snipe and short-eared owl.

At Pasture End our path takes us under the bypass and passes the former trackbed of the Stainmore trans-Pennine Railway. This was a branch line of the South Durham and Lancashire Union Railway. It opened in 1862 and linked Darlington and Barnard Castle with Tebay. Before its closure in 1962 this was the highest railway in England with a maximum elevation of 1370 feet (418m) at the Stainmore summit.

Our route leads down to the river Greta where we cross God's Bridge. Here a huge slab of limestone spans the channel which the Greta has carved out for itself. God's Bridge has wonderful character, with a span of about sixteen feet (5m), and of sufficient width to enable it to be used as a crossing for a drovers' road. Unless in spate, the river sinks underground just below the bridge, reappearing further downstream.

From God's Bridge we have a choice of routes; either the public right of way; or under the Countryside Stewardship Scheme we can now continue along the banks of the Greta. Both routes lead to East Meltwaters Farm. This farm has been sensitively managed for many years and the hay meadows bear witness to this with the increasing variety of plants and flowers. There is also much historical interest on the farm, including a Grade II listed packhorse bridge.

During our return to Bowes we pass the confluence of the river Greta and Sleightholme Beck and there are good views of the castle. The last mile hugs the riverside and a slight detour to see the spectacular Mill Force is recommended.

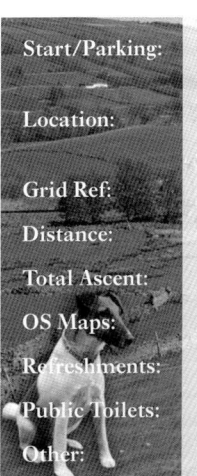

Start/Parking:	Bowes, in the layby just outside the village to the east or in the Parish Hall car park, left of the mini-roundabout.
Location:	Bowes is situated 15½ miles (25km) west of Scotch Corner off the A66 road and 5 miles (8km) from Barnard Castle.
Grid Ref:	NY 997 134. Postcode: DL12 9HU.
Distance:	8 miles (12.9km) circular. Allow 4 hrs walking time.
Total Ascent:	441 feet (134m) Maximum Elevation: 1195 feet (364m).
OS Maps:	Explorer OL31 (1:25,000) or Landranger 92 (1:50,000).
Refreshments:	The Ancient Unicorn in Bowes.
Public Toilets:	None en route, nearest Barnard Castle.
Other:	Post Office, telephone, bus service.

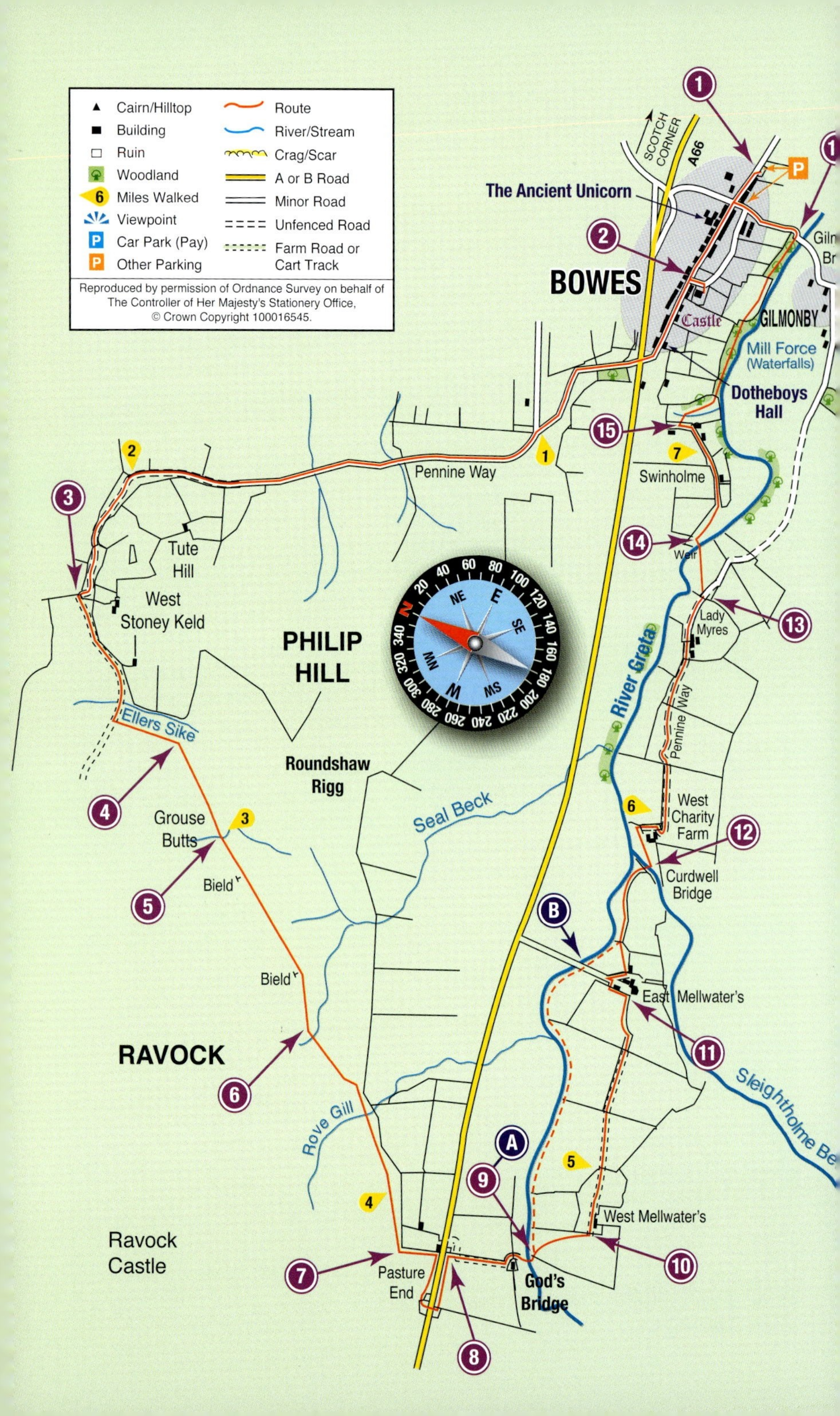

Cairn/Hilltop
Building
Ruin
Woodland
Miles Walked
Viewpoint
Car Park (Pay)
Other Parking
Route
River/Stream
Crag/Scar
A or B Road
Minor Road
Unfenced Road
Farm Road or Cart Track
Reproduced by permission of Ordnance Survey on behalf of The Controller of Her Majesty's Stationery Office, © Crown Copyright 100016545.
SCOTCH CORNER
A66
The Ancient Unicorn
BOWES
Castle
GILMONBY
Mill Force (Waterfalls)
Dotheboys Hall
Pennine Way
Swinholme
Weir
Lady Myres
River Greta
Pennine Way
West Charity Farm
Curdwell Bridge
East Mellwater's
Sleightholme Beck
West Mellwater's
God's Bridge
Pasture End
Ravock Castle
RAVOCK
Rove Gill
Bield
Bield
Grouse Butts
Ellers Sike
Roundshaw Rigg
Seal Beck
PHILIP HILL
West Stoney Keld
Tute Hill
NE
E
SE
SW
W
NW
N

Bowes, Deepdale and God's Bridge

1 *(GR: 997 134)* From the parking place walk up the main street through Bowes passing the Ancient Unicorn, the Post Office and St Giles Church.

2 *(GR: 993 135)* Turn left at the church to visit the keep of Bowes Castle. Return to the main street and follow the road out of the village passing Dotheboys Hall. Cross the bridge over the A66 bypass and follow the road to its demise at West Stoney Keld.

3 *(GR: 972 152)* Go through the gate and turn left onto a clear stone track *(SP Pasture End 2m)*. Continue along the track to a waymark post *(just after crossing Ellers Sike)*, turn left leaving the track and climb up to a waymark post on the hill-top.

4 *(GR: 969 146)* Bear right and follow a clear green track through the heather, heading towards another waymark post adjacent to a line of grouse butts.

5 *(GR: 966 144)* Continue straight ahead, passing below a bield *(a short section of wall with a cross wall)*. Keeping roughly to the same level follow a narrow track passing below another bield. After passing two waymarked stones turn left towards a waymark post.

6 *(GR: 960 137)* From the post continue to the wall, turn right and keeping in line with the wall follow a faint track to the wall corner.

7 *(GR: 955 130)* Turn left and descend towards a gate adjacent to the A66. **STOP** at the gate and turn right *(sign Pennine Way via underpass 200 metres)*. Follow the fence round and go through a gate. Descend left and go through the underpass. Go through a gate, turn left through another gate and follow the left wall across the field.

8 *(GR: 956 128)* Turn right *(SP Pennine Way)* and descend a clear track winding down through a gate to cross God's Bridge. Turn left and go through a gate.

9 *(GR: 957 126)* Bear half right *(SP Bowes 2½m)* and climb over the hill towards the wall. Turn right and follow the wall. **(For alternative route see blue panel below).**

10 *(GR: 959 124)* Go through a gate on the left just before West Meltwaters. Continue on a good farm lane through four fields to East Meltwater's.

11 *(GR: 967 126)* Continue along the track and turn right down the side of the barn. Turn right and follow the farm lane to a barn on the left. Go through a gate *(SP Pennine Way)*, bear left and go through a waymarked gate near the river. Continue with the right wall to Curdwell Bridge.

12 *(GR: 972 128)* Cross the footbridge over Sleightholme Beck and head to the left of the farm buildings at West Charity Farm. Go through a gate *(SP Pennine Way)* and pass through the farmyard. A good farm road leads through the fields past Lady Myres Farm.

13 *(GR: 982 130)* Leave the farm road via a gate on the left and descend to the bottom centre of the field to a footbridge. Cross the footbridge.

14 *(GR: 984 131)* Follow the riverbank downstream and then climb up to join an enclosed track leading to Swinholme Farm. The track improves as we pass the farmhouse and becomes a tarmac surface just before going through a gate.

15 *(GR: 987 134)* Cross a wooden step-stile in the right fence, bear right and descend towards the river. Cross a wooden step-stile and follow the riverbank downstream to Gilmonby Bridge, passing above the striking waterfall of Mill Force.

16 *(GR: 996 132)* Turn left and follow the road to Bowes. At the roundabout turn right and return to the parking place.

ALTERNATIVE ROUTE - shown on the map as a broken red line.

A *(GR: 957 126)* Bear left and follow the river Greta downstream. This purpose built path allows wheelchair users to explore the area around Meltwater's.

B *(GR: 968 129)* Go through two gates crossing the farm road. Continue via another gate and follow the right wall to Curdwell Bridge. Now follow directions from point 12.

EGGLESTONE ABBEY and GRETA BRIDGE

FROM EGGLESTONE ABBEY 6½ MILES (10.5KM)

Sir Walter Scott, Charles Dickens and the artists Cotman and Turner are a few of the famous visitors to Teesdale. This walk explores some of the places where they stayed and the scenery that inspired them.

Our walk begins with a tour of Egglestone Abbey, which is sited on a green knoll above a bend of the river Tees. The abbey was founded c.1195 by the Premonstratensian Canons or the White Canons as they were better known in England, due to the colour of their habits. They were regular canons, not monks, and followed the rule of St Augustine, but they observed a stricter code of austerity similar to the Cistercian order.

The abbey was dissolved in 1540 and some of the buildings were converted into a private residence. Shortly afterwards the church tower was pulled down because it spoiled the view from the house. Some of the stonework was used to pave the stable yard at Rokeby Hall in the nineteenth century.

The remains include a large section of the nave and chancel walls standing almost to their original height. The church floor has a number of tombstones, some bearing inscriptions and the symbols of office. The most impressive of these memorials is the large box-tomb of Sir Ralph Bowes of Streatlam, who died in 1482. It is elaborately sculptured with leafy niches and shields, but unfortunately the cover is missing. The tomb had been removed to the woods behind Mortham Tower where it had been neglected for centuries. It was given back to the abbey in 1929.

From the abbey our route leads to Abbey Bridge where we descend to the banks of the river Tees. The bridge, a wonderful structure with inspired battlements, spans the river via a single arch 76 feet (23m) across. Since its construction in 1773, the bridge has been a popular subject for artists, including Turner who painted it on several occasions.

We continue downstream to the Meeting of the Waters of which Sir Walter Scott enthused; 'The two most beautiful and rapid rivers of the north, Greta and Tees, join current in the demesne.' Just above this confluence is Dairy Bridge with its high, single arch smothered by ivy. Upstream the Greta tumbles down through a deep tree-shaded gorge, both enchanting and beautiful.

Further along the track we pass Mortham Tower, a fifteenth-century pele tower, or border fortress. It was built by the Rokeby family, following the destruction of their former home by Scottish raiders. The tower is four storeys high with parapets and overhanging corner turrets. The other buildings are arranged around three sides of the courtyard with an arched gateway in the south wall to form a barnekin, a walled enclosure where cattle could be protected from border thieves.

After passing under the A66 trunk road we soon arrive at the picturesque village of Greta Bridge. Here an elegant bridge, designed by John Carr, Yorkshire's bridgemaster, crosses the river Greta. The bridge was built in 1789 to replace one that had been destroyed in the 1771 flood. It has a single span of 75 feet (22.7m) with stone balustraded parapets. There is a narrow passage through the west abutment for people and animals to pass.

Greta Bridge was an important place in the old coaching days when it had three inns to cater for the needs of travellers. Charles Dickens, accompanied by his illustrator, Hablot K. Browne 'Phiz', spent the night of 31st January 1838 here after an arduous journey on the mail coach from London. They stayed at the George Inn, now a private house, where Dickens wrote to his wife, expressing his delight at the comforts of the inn and the extent of its breakfast menu.

Leaving Greta Bridge we follow the river upstream to the ruinous old church of St Mary. The ruins date from the thirteenth century, although a fragment of an Anglo-Saxon cross suggests that an earlier church existed on this site. After being dismantled in 1833 much of the stone was used to build a new church in Brignall village. Brignall is believed to take its name from the Saxon *briggen* and *ald*, meaning old-bridge. The village overlooks the broad expanse of northern Teesdale and on a clear day the panorama extends across to the Cleveland Hills.

From Brignall we descend to cross the busy A66 to enter the churchyard of St Mary's at Rokeby. Parish registers show that John Carr was commissioned to complete the building. It was consecrated in 1776, but served without a chancel until 1877. We continue via lush meadows, returning to the road which we follow back to Egglestone Abbey.

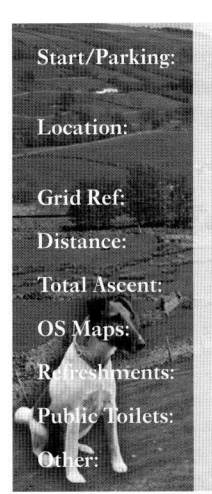

Start/Parking:	Car park at Egglestone Abbey. There are several other parking places along the route (see map).
Location:	Egglestone Abbey is situated 2¼ miles (3.6km) south-east of Barnard Castle, on a minor road off the B6277.
Grid Ref:	NZ 062 150. Postcode: DL12 9TN.
Distance:	6½ miles (10.5km) circular. Allow 4hrs walking time.
Total Ascent:	776 feet (237m) Maximum Elevation: 683 feet (208m).
OS Maps:	Explorer OL31 (1:25,000) or Landranger 92 (1:50,000).
Refreshments:	The Morritt Arms at Greta Bridge.
Public Toilets:	None en route, nearest Barnard Castle.
Other:	Rokeby Park.

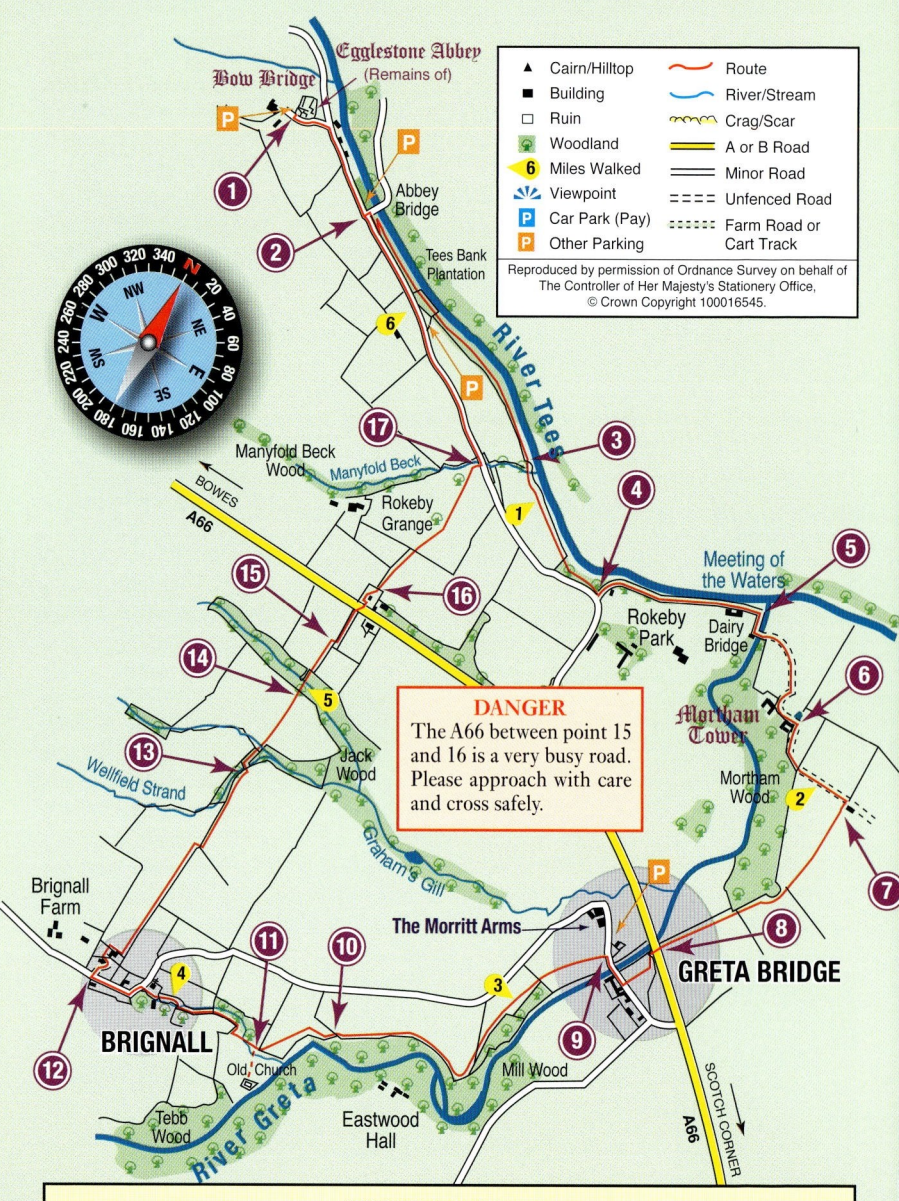

MORTHAM DOBBY

Mortham Tower is said to have been the scene of the murder of a local woman, some centuries ago. Others say that she was shot by robbers while walking in the woods and managed to reach the tower before dying on the steps. Her headless ghost, known as the Mortham Dobby, appears dressed as a fine lady, with a piece of silk trailing behind her. *(No tradition mentions how her head and torso became separated)*. The parson spoke in Latin to her apparition, confining it to the stones under Dairy Bridge. However, the bridge was destroyed by floods in 1771, releasing her spirit to roam once more!

DANGER
The A66 between point 15 and 16 is a very busy road. Please approach with care and cross safely.

Egglestone Abbey and Greta Bridge

① *(GR: 062 150)* From the abbey turn left and follow the road downhill to the junction. Turn right and continue along the road to Abbey Bridge.

② *(GR: 066 149)* Leave the road and follow a narrow path *(SP Teesdale Way Public Footpath)*. After a few yards the path doubles back towards the bridge *(giving a good view of the arch)*. Continue downstream along a good path passing through two gates.

③ *(GR: 075 144)* Go over a step-stile *(doggie friendly)*, Cross a stream and climb up some steps leading into a large field. Turn left and follow the left boundary. Go over another step-stile, bear right and follow a clear path to a gate.

④ *(GR: 079 142)* Go through the gate and turn left onto a private lane *(SP Teesdale Way)*. Follow the lane to the Meeting of the Waters. For a better view you will need to descend along a narrow path to the left and afterwards retrace your steps to the lane.

⑤ *(GR: 084 144)* Continue along the lane to cross Dairy Bridge. Go over a stile to the right of the gate/cattle grid. Follow the lane round to the right and pass to the left of Mortham Tower joining a rough track. Cross a stile to the right of a pond.

⑥ *(GR: 087 142)* Turn right and follow the right boundary to a gate/stile. Cross the stile and follow a rough farm track which leads uphill to a barn.

⑦ *(GR: 090 141)* Turn right and continue directly across the field. Climb up and go through a gate. After crossing over the ridge the A66 comes into view. Follow the right wall and descend through a gate. Continue along the right fence to another gate.

⑧ *(GR: 087 133)* Go through the gate and pass beneath the A66. Climb up to the left and go through a gate. Continue in line with the right boundary through the field to a stone stile leading onto the road. Turn right and follow the road over Greta Bridge.

⑨ *(GR: 086 132)* A few yards after crossing the bridge leave the road via an unusual stile in the left wall *(SP Public Footpath)* and descend some steps into the field. Continue across the field and go over a step-stile. Bear half right and climb up to join a faint path. Follow the left boundary through two fields.

⑩ *(GR: 079 125)* Cross a step-stile and descend to cross a small stream. Climb back up slightly and go through an open gateway in the right wall corner. The ruins of the old church of St Mary are visible to the south and a short diversion can be made to visit them. Then retrace your steps and follow instructions given from point 11.

⑪ *(GR: 077 123)* Turn right *(SP Brignall Village)*. Follow a clear path uphill. On reaching a fence turn right and follow it round to a kissing gate. Go through the gate and follow a fenced path. Turn right and then left, passing to the left of St Mary's Church. Go through a gate beside the church, turn left and follow the road to Brookside.

⑫ *(GR: 071 122)* Turn right *(SP Public Footpath)*. Follow the drive to the right of the cottage and go through a gate behind. Pass to the left of the barn and go through the gate behind it. Head towards the right boundary and follow it, descending gradually. Go through a gap in the fence *(waymark)*. Turn left and follow the left boundary.

⑬ *(GR: 072 131)* Go through a gap in the left boundary *(waymark)* and follow a narrow path down to cross a small stream. Turn right and continue along a fenced path leading into a large field. Go straight across the field.

⑭ *(GR: 072 134)* Continue into the wood *(waymark)* and descend to cross a footbridge. Climb back up and cross a step-stile. Follow the right boundary to a step-stile.

⑮ *(GR: 072 136)* Cross the stile *(waymark)* turn left and follow a narrow fenced path. Cross another step-stile and climb up to the A66. **THIS IS A VERY BUSY ROAD**. Cross the road and turn right for a few yards. Go through the gate on the left and enter the churchyard *(SP Public Footpath)*. Continue round to the back of the church.

⑯ *(GR: 072 138)* Cross a step-stile in the hedge and follow the left boundary, descending gradually. Go over another stile and continue descending to a step-stile.

⑰ *(GR: 074 144)* Cross the stile and turn left onto the road. Follow the road back to Egglestone Abbey.

SUDBURN BECK and STAINDROP MOOR

FROM STAINDROP 7¼ MILES (11.7KM)

This gentle walk wanders through the pastoral countryside around Staindrop. It leads through lush meadows to the boundaries of Streatlam Park and returns alongside the perimeter wall of Raby Park.

Staindrop is a picturesque village built around a network of interlocking greens lined with fine Georgian houses. It was recorded as 'Standropa' in 1050 and derives from the Old English *staener-hop*, which translates to stoney valley. The village was first mentioned *c.*1031, after King Cnut undertook a barefooted pilgrimage to the shrine of St Cuthbert at Durham. There, stripped of every symbol of royalty, he knelt humbly before the shrine and bestowed on the church a gift of the manor of Staindrop, along with many other estates.

To the eastern end of the village stands the Church of St Mary which dates back to the eighth century. Traces of the original Anglo-Saxon windows are visible in the nave above the later Norman arches. The south aisle boasts a wonderful set of Decorated piscina, sedilia and tomb arch. The rood screen is pre-Reformation, the only surviving example in County Durham. However, these features are overshadowed by the magnificence of the monuments to the Lords of Raby. St. Mary's has the distinction of being the last English parish church to celebrate the Roman Mass in Latin. This took place at the Rising of the North in 1569.

Leaving Staindrop our route leads through the meadows to Sudburn Beck which guides us upstream, past Snotterton Hall. This was the site of the old fortified manor house of Snotterton. It was demolished in 1831 and rebuilt as a farmhouse. The old hall was built in the fifteenth century. Several of its windows were triple mullioned and the walls had an embattled parapet, with crocketed pinnacles at the angles. The present house incorporates remnants of the old structure; these include a mullioned window in the south-eastern corner of the courtyard and the remains of a crocketed pinnacle on the roof of the west range of the buildings.

Our route continues along the delightful Sudburn Beck to the boundary of Streatlam Park. These walls once enclosed the estate of Streatlam Castle, an impressive Baroque stately home belonging to the Bowes-Lyon family. The estate was sold in 1922, allegedly to pay for the costs of the wedding of Lady Elizabeth Bowes-Lyon to HRH The Duke of York. In 1927, the new owner auctioned everything of value and pulled down the mansion, leaving the fifteenth century shell of the castle exposed. These remains were blown up in 1959, as part of a Territorial Army exercise.

In 1558, Sir George Bowes of Streatlam pledged loyalty to Queen Elizabeth I when she ascended to the throne. However, Charles Nevill, the Earl of Westmorland who lived at Raby Castle, was allied to the Catholic cause. Nevill joined with Thomas Percy, the Earl of Northumberland, to lead the ill fated rebellion in support of Mary, Queen of Scots. In November 1569, 700 knights assembled in the Baron's Hall at Raby Castle, where they plotted the Rising of the North.

When the rebels advanced on Streatlam, Sir George made a strategic withdrawal to Barnard Castle which was easier to defend. Nevill laid siege to the castle and Sir George held out for eleven days until being forced to surrender after the water supply had been cut off. But, this delay proved very costly to the rebels, it bought the Crown enough time to march their army north and put down the rebellion.

Nevill escaped to Holland where he died penniless in 1601. He was attainted for treason and his estates were forfeited to the Crown. Percy was less fortunate. He was captured by the Scottish Regent and ransomed to Queen Elizabeth in 1572. He was taken to York and, without the formality of a trial, beheaded in a public execution. His head was placed on a spike above Micklegate Bar, where it remained for about two years before being removed by sympathisers. He was beatified by Leo XIII on 13 May, 1895.

The pastoral landscape of Staindrop Moor provides the ideal habitat for the kestrel, easily identified by its hovering flight as it watches for small mammals in the fields below. Kestrels remain almost stationary by flying into the wind, hence its other name – the windhover. Other birds to watch out for include goldcrest, linnet, skylark, snipe, yellow hammer and wheatear.

After returning to the main road our route follows the high wall of Raby Park and re-enters Staindrop via an ancient track known as Knicky Nack Lane.

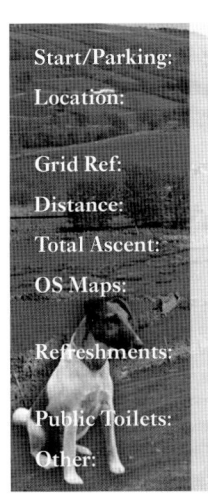

Start/Parking:	Staindrop, adjacent to the village green.
Location:	Staindrop is 6 miles (9.6km) north-east of Barnard Castle on the A688 and 11½ miles (18.6Km) west of Darlington along the B6729.
Grid Ref:	NZ 128 206. Postcode: DL2 3LD.
Distance:	7¼ miles (11.7km) circular. Allow 3½ hrs walking time.
Total Ascent:	549 feet (167m) Maximum Elevation: 626 feet (191m).
OS Maps:	Explorer OL31, 304 and 305 (1:25,000) due to OS divisions or the complete route on Landranger 92 (1:50,000).
Refreshments:	The Black Swan, the Royal Oak Inn and the Wheatsheaf Inn at Staindrop.
Public Toilets:	Staindrop, none en route.
Other:	Post Office, shops, fish and chip shop, bus service, telephone.

KINNINVIE
B6279
High House
Friar Cote
Bolton Hill
Lingberry Quarry
Forthburn Beck
Streatlam Park
Woodend Farm
Great Wood
STAINDROP MOOR
Moor Lane
Ladyclose Wood
West Lodge
Streatlam Grove
Scaife House
Blakeley
Raby Park
Snotterton Hall
BARNARD CASTLE
A688
Moor Beck
Langley Beck
Moor Close Farm
Sudburn Bridge
Sudburn Beck
Cleatlam Bridge
STAINDROP
B6274
1
2
3
4
5
6
7
8
9
10
11
12
13
14
15
16
Cairn/Hilltop
Building
Ruin
Woodland
Miles Walked
Viewpoint
Car Park (Pay)
Other Parking
Route
River/Stream
Crag/Scar
A or B Road
Minor Road
Unfenced Road
Farm Road or Cart Track
Reproduced by permission of Ordnance Survey on behalf of The Controller of Her Majesty's Stationery Office, © Crown Copyright 100016545.

Sudburn Beck and Staindrop Moor

(1) *(GR: 128 206)* Locate Stangarth Lane at the side of the Scarth Memorial Hall. Follow the lane *(SP Pubic Footpath)* to Nursery Garage.

(2) *(GR: 128 204)* Turn right and continue to the end of the lane. Cross a wooden step-stile and bear left slightly to reach a step-stile. Go over the stile and then cross a stone bridge, continue ahead and go through a stile in the hedge opposite. Bear half right and head towards the far right corner of the field at Cleatlam Bridge.

(3) *(GR: 124 199)* Go over a step-stile in the hedge, cross the road and go over another stile *(SP Public Footpath)*. Now follow the course of Sudburn Beck through the meadows to Sudburn Bridge.

(4) *(GR: 116 198)* Cross the stile, climb some steps and continue across the A688 road, *(also cross a small section of the former A688)*. Go through a stile and continue straight ahead to cross a wooden stile. Follow the course of Sudburn Beck, which bears sharp left at point 5.

(5) *(GR: 114 198)* Cross a wooden stile on the left. Continue along the side of Sudburn Beck, passing below Snotterton Hall to reach Streatlam Grove.

(6) *(GR: 102 198)* Go over a wooden stile and cross a rough farm road and continue through a gate. Leave the beckside and climb up towards the farm buildings. Pass to the left of the barns and go through a stile. Descend to the beck and continue alongside it to Woodend Farm.

(7) *(GR: 095 197)* Bear right slightly and pass in front of the cottage, go through two stiles, crossing a farm road. Continue straight ahead, pass through a hedge and climb to reach a gate in a stone wall. *(This is the boundary wall of Streatlam Park)*.

(8) *(GR: 092 197)* Turn right and follow the wall uphill through four fenced fields to reach a gate in the wall corner.

(9) *(GR: 088 201)* Go through the gate and head diagonally across the field to a stile in the top right corner.

(10) *(GR: 084 203)* Cross the stile and descend via a gate and a stile to the former Lingberry Quarry. Join a rough track and follow the field boundary to a gate.

(11) *(GR: 087 207)* Go through the gate and follow the farm track uphill to Friar Cote. Continue through a gate and follow the lane down to the B6279 road.

(12) *(GR: 089 213)* Turn right and continue along the B6279 road for approximately half a mile (800m).

(13) *(GR: 097 210)* Turn left and leave the road *(SP Public Footpath)*. Cross a cattle grid and follow the lane down to another cattle grid. Leave the lane via the stile on the right. Now keep to the wallside through several large fields, passing two lodges.

(14) *(GR: 116 206)* Bear right towards the bottom corner of the field. Cross a stone step-stile and then follow the right boundary through the field. Cross a wooden step-stile and continue along the right boundary.

(15) *(GR: 121 205)* Cross a wooden step-stile on the left and join a fenced path. Follow the path onto a walled lane, known as Knicky Nack Lane. Continue to the end of this lane which leads to Staindrop.

(16) *(GR: 124 205)* Continue along the main street to your starting point. If time allows you may wish to visit St Mary's Church.

RABY CASTLE

Raby Castle was built in the mid-fourteenth century by the mighty Nevill family. It is one of the grandest medieval castles in England, surrounded by a magnificent deer park, lake and walled gardens. The castle consists of nine perimeter towers, the largest of these is Clifford's Tower, 81 feet (24.7 m) tall. The Kitchen Tower has remained relatively unchanged since medieval times. The Baron's Hall is most magnificent, this was where 700 knights assembled to plot the Rising of the North rebellion.

Glossary

Most of the local place-names are Anglo-Saxon or Norse in origin. They were made up from words used in everyday speech and described one particular spot, clearly defining it from other places in the immediate neighbourhood. Anglo-Saxon names include those ending with *ing, ley, ham* and *ton*. Norse names include those ending with *by, sett* and *thwaite*. The Normans had a smaller influence on place-names, being confined to changes in the spelling of existing names. They gave us the Domesday Book in 1086 recording the name, population and value of each village.

Baldersdale:	*Baldhere's valley.*
Barnard Castle:	*Castle of Baron Bernard.*
Barningham:	*The settlement of the people of Beorna.*
Blackton:	*Black valley.*
Boldron:	*Forest-clearing where steers were kept.*
Bowes:	*The river-bends.*
Brignall:	*Nook of land belonging to the Brynings.*
Briscoe:	*Birch wood.*
Cleatlam:	*Clearing where burdock grows.*
Cotherstone:	*Cuthere's farm.*
Cronkley:	*Crooked cliff.*
Darlington:	*Deornoth's peoples' settlement.*
Deepdale:	*Deep valley.*
Durham:	*Island with a hill.*
Eggleston::	*Egills farm.*
Gilmonby:	*Gilman's farm.*
Goldsborough:	*Stronghold of a man called Godel.*
Grassholme:	*Grassy island.*
Greta Bridge:	*Bridge over the stony stream.*
Hamsterley:	*Corn-weevil meadow.*
Holwick:	*The ravine in the hollow.*
Hunderthwaite:	*Huenders clearing.*
Greta Bridge:	*Bridge over the stony stream.*
Langdon Beck:	*Long hill near the beck.*
Lartington:	*Lyrta's farm.*
Lonton:	*Farm near the Lune.*
Lunedale:	*Valley of the Lune.*
Mickleton:	*Large farm.*
Middleton-in-Teesdale:	*Middle settlement in Teesdale.*
Mortham :	*Morta's homestead.*
Newbiggin:	*New building* or *dwelling.*
Raby:	*Village* or *homestead near the boundary mark.*
River Balder:	*Baldhere's river.*
River Greta:	*The stony stream.*
River Lune:	*Clean, pure or healthy river.*
River Tees:	*Boiling* or *surging river.*
Rokeby:	*Hroca's farm.*
Romaldkirk:	*Church dedicated to St Rumold.*
Selset:	*Seli's pasture.*
Shackleborough:	*The hill with a pole on top.*
Sleightholme:	*Level raised ground.*
Snotterton:	*Snytra's farm.*
Staindrop:	*Valley with stoney ground.*
Stainmoor:	*Rocky moor.*
Startforth:	*Ford where Watling Street crosses the river Tees.*
Streatlam:	*Clearing by the Roman road.*
Stony Keld:	*Spring by the rocky mound.*
Whorlton:	*Farm by the millstream.*

Some other topographical terms

beck:	*A small stream.*
birk(s):	*Birch tree or wood.*
burn:	*Stream.*
cote:	*A cottage or shelter.*
garth:	*An enclosure, paddock or yard.*
gill:	*A ravine, a narrow valley with a stream.*
hagg:	*A part or division of a wood.*
helm:	*A cattle shelter or hut.*
holm(e):	*A water meadow, the land within the bend of a stream.*
how(e):	*A mound or small hill.*
ing(s):	*A meadow or pasture.*
keld:	*A spring.*
rigg:	*A ridge, long narrow hill.*
scar:	*Escarpment, cliff or outcrop.*
thorpe:	*An outlying farm or hamlet.*
thwaite:	*A clearing in woodland.*

The Country Code

Enjoy the countryside and respect its life and works	Keep to public paths across farmland	Leave livestock, crops and farm machinery alone	Use gates and stiles to cross fences, hedges and walls
Guard against all risks of fire	Make no unnecessary noise	Leave all gates as you find them	Take your litter home
Help to keep all water clean	Protect wildlife, plants and trees	Take special care on country roads	Keep dogs under close control

Also . . .

Use car parks where possible and park with consideration for village residents and other road users.

Don't obstruct farm gates, tracks or entrances.

When walking on roads, walk on the right hand side to face oncoming traffic. When approaching blind bends, cross to the opposite side to enable you to see and be seen in both directions.

Allow sufficient time to complete the walk in daylight hours, and be sure to be off the fells by dusk.

Let others know the route you have taken, the time you expect to return and stick to the route.

If the weather turns nasty and you decide to quit the walk or take shelter in a hostelry etc, be sure to let others know so they do not worry and call out the emergency services unnecessarily.

Information Desk

ABBEYS

Egglestone Abbey, near Barnard Castle.
The ruins of a small monastery of Premonstratensian White Canons, picturesquely set above a bend in the river Tees near Barnard Castle. The remains include much of the thirteenth-century church and a range of living quarters, with traces of their ingenious toilet drainage system.

CASTLES

Barnard Castle, Barnard Castle.
Set on a high rock above the river Tees, on the fringe of an attractive market town. Barnard Castle takes its name from its twelfth-century founder, Bernard de Balliol, this imposing fortress was later developed by Richard III.

Bowes Castle, Bowes.
The impressive remains of Henry II's twelfth-century keep, on the site of a Roman fort which once guarded the approach to the strategic Stainmore Pass over the Pennines. It was a solitary keep without the protection of curtain walls. A rectangular ditch enclosure was its only outer defence.

HISTORIC HOUSES and GARDENS

Raby Castle, Staindrop.
One of the most impressive inhabited castles in England. Built in the mid-fourteenth century, the castle sits amongst 200 acres of beautiful parkland containing herds of deer.

Rokeby Park, near Barnard Castle.
Palladian style country house. The setting for Sir Walter Scott's ballad 'Rokeby'. It holds a collection of period furniture and eighteenth-century needle painting pictures.

Eggleston Hall Gardens, Eggleston.
Four acres of walled gardens within the grounds of Eggleston Hall. A plantsman's garden with many rare and unusual plants.

MARKET DAYS

Barnard Castle, Wednesday.
At the time of going to print Barnard Castle also held a farmers' market 10am to 3pm on the first Saturday of every month and Middleton-in-Teesdale held a farmers' market 11am to 4pm on the last Sunday of each month from April to September.

MUSEUMS

Bowes Museum, Barnard Castle.
The Bowes Museum offers a fascinating museum experience for all the family. It contains one of the finest collections of European fine and decorative arts in the North of England and an acclaimed exhibition programme, alongside special events and children's activities.

NATURAL FEATURES

Cauldron Snout, Cow Green Reservoir.
Here the river Tees plunges, in a series of cataracts, down a rocky staircase 200 yards (180m) in length, with a vertical drop of 200 feet (60m) from the first cataract to the last. England's highest cascade waterfall.

Gibson's Cave, Bowlees.
Gibson's Cave, reputedly where an outlaw of that name went to hide from the law. It was created by the erosion of Summerhill Falls, whose own erosion created a shelf behind the actual waterfall.

High Force, near Middleton-in-Teesdale.
One of England's most spectacular waterfalls. High Force thunders 70 feet (21m) over the Whin Sill volcanic rock into a deep pool below. In turmoil High Force has been known to engulf the central rock in a single waterfall.

NATURE RESERVES

Moor House, Langdon Beck.
England's highest and largest terrestrial National Nature Reserve (NNR), a UNESCO Biosphere Reserve and a European Special Protection Area. Habitats include exposed summits, extensive blanket peatlands, upland grasslands, pastures, hay meadows and deciduous woodland.

Hamsterley Forest, near Bishop Auckland.
Hamsterley is a delightful oasis of broadleaved and coniferous woodland, spread along the sides of a sheltered valley. With waymarked walks, cycle routes and horse riding trails.

Hannah's Meadow, Baldersdale, near Cotherstone.
These fields were farmed by Hannah Hauxwell using traditional methods, without the use of artificial fertilisers. One of the barns has been converted to an un-manned visitors centre with displays and information.

PETROL STATIONS

Barnard Castle, Eggleston, Mickleton, Middleton-in-Teesdale.

PONY TREKKING and RIDING

Raygill Riding Centre, Lartington.

TOURIST INFORMATION

Barnard Castle TIC.
Bowlees Visitor Centre.
Grassholme Reservoir Visitor Centre.
Hamsterley Forest Visitor Centre.
Middleton-in-Teesdale TIC.

VETERINARY SURGERIES

Castle Veterinary Surgeons, Barnard Castle.
Wilsons Veterinary Group, Bishop Auckland.
Fellside Veterinary Group, Stanhope.

YOUTH HOSTELS

Baldersdale, Youth Hostel.
Holwick, Camping Barn.
Langdon Beck, Youth Hostel.

WATERSPORTS

Angling, the river Tees and all six reservoirs.
Canoeing, the river Tees below High Force.
Sailing, Grassholme Reservoir.
Swimming, Teesdale Sports Centre, Barnard Castle.
Walter Skiing, Balderhead Reservoir.
Wind Surfing, Selset Reservoir.
Information on permits/restrictions for the above activities obtainable from Tourist Information Centres.